INVINCIBLE WARRIOR

合気道開祖 植芝 盛平翁

The Invincible Warrior, Morihei Ueshiba (1883–1969),
Founder of Aikido

INVINCIBLE
WARRIOR

A N I L L U S T R A T E D
B I O G R A P H Y O F
M O R I H E I U E S H I B A ,
F O U N D E R O F A I K I D O

J O H N S T E V E N S

S H A M B H A L A
Boston & London
1997

Shambhala Publications, Inc.
Horticultural Hall
300 Massachusetts Avenue
Boston, Massachusetts 02115
http://www.Shambhala.com

9 8 7 6 5 4 3 2 1

Designed by Ruth Kolbert

First Edition

Printed in the United States of America

⊗ This edition is printed on acid-free paper that meets
the American National Standards Institute Z39.48 Standard.

Distributed in the United States by Random House, Inc.,
and in Canada by Random House of Canada Ltd

Library of Congress Cataloging-in-Publication Data
Stevens, John, 1947–
    Invincible warrior: an illustrated biography of Morihei
Ueshiba, founder of Aikido/John Stevens.—1st ed.
        p.   cm.
    Includes bibliographical references and index.
    ISBN 1–57062–075–X (cloth: alk. paper)
    1. Ueshiba, Morihei, 1883–1969. 2. Martial artists—
Japan—Biography. 3. Aikido. I. Title.
GV1113.U37S955   1997
796.8'092—dc21
[B]   97-9234
                                                    CIP

CONTENTS

Preface

Invincible Warrior tells the fascinating life story of Morihei Ueshiba, likely the greatest of martial artists and a grand visionary whose quest for the true meaning of warriorship led to the creation of Aikido, "The Art of Peace," a progressive and enlightened discipline practiced all over the globe. *Invincible Warrior* is a traditional biography that covers the three factors involved in Morihei's life: the outer factors (places, dates, teachers); the inner factors (purpose and nature of his quest); and the secret factors (his mystical experiences and spiritual accomplishments). Part I: The Life and Times of Morihei Ueshiba, is a revised and expanded version of material that originally appeared in *Abundant Peace: Morihei Ueshiba, Founder of Aikido*. This section concentrates on the people, events, and ideas that most influenced him. Part II: Morihei Ueshiba and the Creation of Aikido, is a visual documentation of his amazing career, from his youth to his final years. Part III, The Marvelous Techniques of Morihei Ueshiba, presents Morihei's prewar Aiki Budo and postwar Aikido techniques. Taken together, the three parts of this biography should paint an accurate portrait of Morihei Ueshiba, the invincible warrior.

I have focused exclusively on Morihei in this biography, and have not mentioned, except in passing, his many outstanding and colorful disciples. Their interesting tales should be told, but such material belongs more properly to a much broader survey of the "History of Aikido."

Japanese names are given in the Western format, family name last. In Japan, outstanding figures are often referred to by their first names. In this book, I refer to the following masters by their first names: Morihei Ueshiba, Kumagusu Minakata, Sokaku Takeda, Nao Deguchi, and Onisaburo Deguchi. All Japanese martial arts—Aiki Budo, Aikido, Budo, Judo, Jujutsu, Karate, Kendo, Sumo—are capitalized as proper nouns. Words such as dojo (training hall), which have become familiar to Western readers, are not printed in italics but all other Japanese terms are at the first occurrence.

ACKNOWLEDGMENTS

I am very grateful to Kisshomaru Ueshiba for permission to reproduce photographs from the Ueshiba family collection, to Alan Nagahisa for providing photographs taken of Morihei when the master visited Hawaii in 1961, and to Charles Hill for photographs taken in Tanabe and Kumano, Japan. Heartfelt thanks go to Peter Turner, David O'Neal, and Emily Bower of Shambhala Publications for their hard work on this project, and to my family, friends, and students for their constant support and encouragement.

PART ONE

THE
LIFE
AND TIMES
OF
MORIHEI UESHIBA

MORIHEI UESHIBA WAS BORN ON DECEMBER 14, 1883 (November 16 according to the old lunar calendar) in the castle town of Tanabe, Japan. Tanabe, about two hundred miles south of Osaka, is located along the coast of the Province of Kii (present-day Wakayama Prefecture) and lies at the foot of the Kumano Mountains. Kumano is Japan's Holy Land, the sacred place where the Shinto gods descended to earth; the gateway to Amida Buddha's Pure Land is also believed to be hidden there. The entire district of Kumano is venerated as a mountain mandala—home, over the centuries, to a host of ascetics, wonder-workers, and sages who thrived on the pure air, fresh spring water, succulent fruit, and medicinal herbs of that blessed place and who refreshed body and soul in the soothing hot springs that dot the landscape. The grand shrines of Kumano and the sacred waterfall of Nachi are the meccas of Shinto, and every Japanese true believer, including the emperor, longs to make at least one pilgrimage to worship at those sacred sites and perhaps catch a glimpse of one of the Eight Great Dragon Kings who sport in the Nachi Falls. The Buddhist mecca of Mount Koya is also found in Kii. Kobo Daishi, patriarch of Tantric

Buddhism in Japan, entered eternal meditation on Mount Koya more than a thousand years ago, but he remains a living presence in the area—even today worthy souls are believed capable of catching a glimpse of the Great Master as he endlessly circles the pilgrim trail. Centuries ago, En-no-Gyoja, the Grand Wizard, practiced Taoist meditation techniques in the surrounding mountains and used his magic to fly from peak to peak; modern-day *yamabushi* (mountain ascetics) insist that En-no-Gyoja appears to them in vivid visions. It is said that colors and sounds can be perceived in their original state in Kumano, and that ascetic practices conducted there result in unparalleled clarity of mind and clairvoyance. In the year of Morihei's birth one such yamabushi named Jitsukage leapt from the top of towering Nachi Falls as a final act of *sutemi-gyo,* the total abandonment of body and soul to the Divine. From birth, Morihei was immersed in an atmosphere in which the supernatural, the mysterious, and the holy were palpably present.

The people of Kii are very pious but they are far from being dreamy mystics indifferent to the affairs of the world. Many of them were extraordinary entrepreneurs, epitomized by the eighteenth-century merchant Kinokuniya Bunzaemon. Bunzaemon became fabulously wealthy by cornering first the mandarin orange market and then the timber market. However, the motto of Kii merchants was "earn much; spend much," and Bunzaemon went through his entire fortune and died penniless. Morihei, who received a sizable inheritance from his father, was at times quite well-off, yet he too displayed a cavalier attitude toward money throughout his life and left behind few material possessions.

The town of Tanabe is situated along the Pacific Ocean, warmed by favorable currents; the sea is generally calm and the weather sunny. On occasion, violent storms blow up suddenly, rage frightfully for a time, and then quickly pass. The people of Tanabe are noted for fearful outbursts of anger that, fortunately, also dissipate quickly, and they are further characterized as being headstrong and stubborn. In this regard, Morihei remained a true son of Tanabe all his days.

Already parents to three daughters, Morihei's father and mother were delighted by the birth of their first son, considering him a gift of the Kumano gods, who finally answered their fervent prayers for a baby boy. (They had one more child, another daughter.) A prosperous landowner and longtime town councilman (he served on the council for eighteen years), Morihei's father, Yoroku, was of sturdy samurai stock and solid build. He inherited these traits from his grandfather, Kichiemon, the founder of the Ueshiba clan, once renowned throughout Japan for his size and prodigious strength. Morihei's mother, Yuki—distantly related to the Takeda clan, one of the greatest samurai families—was a cultured and pious woman.

Morihei was apparently born prematurely and was thus rather frail and sickly as a child. Both his parents and his older sisters doted on the boy, though, and he grew into a robust teenager. Morihei spent most of his youth outdoors. At four o'clock each morning his mother would take him along with her as she worshiped at each of the neighborhood shrines. During spring and summer days, Morihei spearfished or swam in the bay; in fall and winter he hiked in the mountains. Around the age of six, Morihei was sent to a nearby temple school. The dry Confucian classics bored him but he was enthralled by the elaborate rituals, mystical chants, visualization exercises, and meditation techniques of esoteric Shingon Buddhism. Morihei displayed an insatiable interest in exoteric science as well, devouring hundreds of books on mathematics, chemistry, and physics.

As he grew older, Morihei awakened to the potential power of his body. In his teens, Morihei began toughening his skin by dousing himself daily with buckets of water and by asking his friends to pelt him with prickly chestnuts. Morihei further increased his strength and stamina by working on fishing boats where he harpooned large fish, hauled in heavy nets, and arm wrestled with powerful young fishermen. Morihei also worked on the docks, where he earned four times the regular wage because he lifted such heavy loads of lumber. Whenever there was a Sumo contest, Morihei was the first to enter, usually emerging as champion. He took special pride in the number of mallets he shattered during village rice cake–pounding ceremonies. To strengthen his legs, Morihei carried ill or aged pilgrims on his back to the main Kumano Shrine, a distance of some fifty miles. Morihei wanted to be strong, strong enough to vanquish the thugs hired by political rivals who harassed his father, strong enough to defeat anyone who challenged him.

Even during this period of intense physical training, Morihei's faith in the spiritual power of traditional religion never wavered; he continued to chant the Shingon mantra he memorized as a boy and to perform ritual purification in the ocean and under waterfalls. A pilgrimage he made with his mother to the Thirty-three Sacred Sites of western Japan was one of the highlights of his teenage years.

In 1896, at the age of thirteen, Morihei was enrolled in the newly opened Tanabe Middle School but within a year he persuaded his parents to let him withdraw. Morihei was too impatient to follow an established curriculum and disliked being confined indoors. He enrolled in an abacus academy and, blessed with a razor-sharp mind and deft hand, was acting as an assistant instructor there in little more than a year.

After graduating from the academy, Morihei took a job as an auditor at the local tax office. He performed his duties well enough to attract the offer of a transfer to the central bureau in Tokyo. Morihei did not want to be a "pencil pusher" the rest of his life, so not only did he refuse the appointment, but he quit his job to work on behalf of hard-pressed fishermen against the recently promulgated Fishery Industries Regulation Act. Certain wealthy operators and corrupt officials were using the law to stifle competition. Indignant, the seventeen-year-old Morihei used his knowledge of the tax codes to defend his neighbors. He also protected them against threats of violent reprisal.

However admirable, Morihei's activism caused his father no small amount of consternation. Yoroku advised his son to seek an occupation that suited him better and offered to stake Morihei on a business venture in Tokyo. Nineteen-year-old Morihei arrived in Tokyo in 1902 and, with the help of one of his rich relatives, he was able to establish a small, thriving stationery business. During this stay in Tokyo, Morihei apparently practiced Tenshin Shin'yo Jujutsu and perhaps Shinkage swordsmanship, his first training in the martial arts. Despite his initial success, Morihei's heart was not in business and city life made him ill. He turned everything over to his employees and was back in Tanabe, empty-handed, by the end of the year. Shortly after his return, Morihei married Hatsu Itogawa, a distant relative.

Morihei's Military Service in Meiji Japan

The Japanese Shogunate collapsed in 1868 and one of the reasons was its inability to resist foreign demands that Japan open its doors to Western trade and influence. Beginning with the Treaty of Kanagawa, signed in 1854, Japan was forced to negotiate a number of unequal treaties with the Western powers, and the new leaders of the Meiji Restoration, intent on avoiding colonization, embarked on a breakneck buildup of the nation's military. By the 1880s, the Meiji government felt strong enough to renegotiate certain treaties and, caught up in the spirit of the times, to attempt some imperialism of its own. Japanese colonial policy was based on European models, a variation on the right of "superior" races to dominate and guide the destinies of "lesser" peoples.

Japan's first target was Korea, which had been bullied by

Japan into agreeing to unequal treaties, much like the ones initially imposed on the Japanese by Western powers. China, which considered Korea a vassal state, objected to Japan's designs there and war broke out between China and Japan in 1894. Much to the world's surprise, Japan—a virtually defenseless group of islands in 1868—soundly defeated China, and in fact could have occupied Peking if it had pressed further. Japan dictated the terms of a highly favorable peace treaty with China in 1895, which alarmed the Western allies, particularly Russia. The Western powers ganged up on Japan and intimidated their new rival into giving up many of the concessions it had obtained from China. Although not strong enough to challenge the Western powers at the time, Japanese military leaders secretly vowed to avenge the humiliation. War with Russia was considered inevitable, and thereafter fifty-five percent of the national budget went to bolster the armed forces. The notion of "Imperial Japan" first gained wide currency around this time, and that phrase was bandied about with increasing fervor over the years to justify Japan's adventurism abroad.

Intoxicated by the victory over China, the Japanese public enthusiastically supported the military buildup. As the rivalry on the continent between Japan and Russia intensified, the threat of full-scale fighting looked imminent. In 1903, Morihei was among the thousands of recruits called up to fortify the nation's reserve forces.

Morihei looked forward to the challenge of military life. However, he failed the initial induction examination because he was shorter than the required minimum height of five feet two inches. Mortified by this rejection, Morihei attached heavy weights to his legs and hung from tree branches for hours to stretch his spine the necessary half inch. Much to his relief, Morihei passed the physical the following year and he was assigned to a regiment stationed in Osaka.

Morihei's Shingon Buddhist master Mitsujo Fujimoto conducted a special fire ceremony for his pupil before he departed for Osaka. This triggered the first of what was to be a long series of mystical experiences for Morihei: "During the ceremony, I felt my guardian deity settling into the core of my being, and I knew that it would protect me wherever I went." Mitsujo also presented Morihei with a Shingon "Seal of Attainment" certificate (similar to the *inka* certificate Zen masters give to disciples who have achieved *satori*).

Fiercely competitive and driven to compensate for his small stature, Morihei excelled at boot camp. Always extraordinarily fleet of foot, Morihei finished at the head of every twenty-five-mile march despite the burden of extra backpacks picked up from stragglers along the way; even officers riding on horses were hard pressed to keep pace with Morihei during those marches. Morihei relentlessly increased his power, astonishing his officers by lifting heavy cannons single-handedly, crushing bamboo between his arms, bending iron rods with his bare hands, and moving enormous boulders. Morihei also quickly emerged as camp Sumo champion and top bayonet fighter. During his military service Morihei was introduced to the basics of Western military science and the use of firearms as well.

Morihei used his head, literally, to make a name for himself in the army. For some years previously, he had toughened his forehead by pounding it against a stone slab a hundred times a day. (This was a common training technique for Sumo wrestlers.) Officers in the old Japanese army were notorious for raining blows down upon the heads of their subordinates for the slightest real or imagined infraction. More than one irascible officer fractured his knuckles on Morihei's rock-hard skull, and big bullies who picked on the diminutive soldier could be knocked unconscious by a head butt. (Fifty years later, during a demonstration, Morihei was struck full force on the head with a wooden sword; despite a tremendous *thunk* observers were amazed to see Morihei laugh off the blow saying, "Nothing can crack this old stone head of mine.") Morihei was greatly admired for his prowess as a fighting machine, but he was considered quite odd for his re-fusal to indulge in another favorite military pastime—regular visits to brothels.

During his tour of duty, Morihei enrolled in the dojo of Masakatsu Nakai in Sakai, a suburb of Osaka, where he learned Goto-ha Yagyu Ryu Jujutsu together with sword and spear fighting. This was Morihei's first systematic study of a classical martial art tradition; he learned how to wield a sword, spear, and *jo* (four-foot wooden staff) with expertise and coordinate weapon movements and body techniques. (Morihei received a teaching license from this school in 1908.) In the Yagyu martial art tradition, mind control is stressed as much as physical technique. In fact, mental power—an unperturbed immovable mind—will always pre-vail over brute strength. A well-known anecdote, told to every Yagyu trainee, goes like this:

> Iemitsu, the third Tokugawa shogun, received a tiger as a gift from the Korean court. The shogun dared the famous swordsman Yagyu Tajima Munenori to subdue the beast. Yagyu immediately accepted the challenge, strode confi-dently into the cage, and whacked the snarling animal on the head with his iron fan just as the tiger was about to pounce. The tiger shrank back and cowered in the corner. The Zen master Takuan, who was also present, chided Yagyu, "That is the wrong approach." Takuan then en-tered the cage unarmed, spat on his hands, and gently rubbed the tiger's face and ears. The ferocious beast calmed down at once, purring and rubbing itself against the monk. Takuan turned to Yagyu and said, "A whack on the head will turn him into an enemy forever; gentle persuasion will make him your friend for life."

The long expected Russo-Japanese War finally erupted in February 1904, when the Japanese navy attacked and trapped the Russian fleet at Port Arthur. Morihei was held back in the reserves even though his regiment was called up.

Insisting that he be sent to the front, Morihei was assigned to a regiment departing for Manchuria. It is not clear how much action Morihei saw there—unbeknownst to Morihei, his father had written to the military authorities requesting that his only son be kept out of danger. For this reason he was given an assignment with the military police away from the front; Morihei did have some harrowing encounters with bandit lords, however, and he had firsthand experience of being under fire.

Upon the conclusion of the Russo-Japanese War in 1905, several of Morihei's superiors recommended a career in the military for the gung-ho soldier, offering to sponsor him as a candidate for the Military Officers Training School. Yoroku was opposed to this course of action for his sole heir and Morihei himself was troubled by what he had witnessed on the battlefield. On the Japanese side, much of the fighting consisted of human wave attacks, which always involve the reckless expenditure of human lives. Many years later, in 1962, Morihei stated in an interview, "I enjoyed being in the military but I innately felt that war is never the solution to any problem. War always means death and destruction and that can never be a good thing." Such an attitude was rare. In defeating Russia, Japan had scored another victory over a much larger country, this time a Western power, and a tide of euphoric nationalism swept over the nation. Distinguished service in the military as an officer was one of highest honors a young man could hope for.

Morihei rejected that course of action, however, and returned to Tanabe as a civilian in 1906. The next few years were very trying for Morihei. He fell into great spiritual torment; he disappeared for days at a time, either by shutting himself up in his room to fast and pray or by hiding out in the mountains, madly swinging his sword for hours and hours. He was uncommunicative with his family and friends and prone to anguished outbursts, so much so that his family worried about his sanity.

During this troubled period Morihei was still able to maintain his martial art training. In addition to his continuing study of the Goto-ha Yagyu Ryu, Morihei practiced a bit of Kodokan Judo at the dojo his father built on family property. In 1909, the twenty-five-year-old Morihei came under the beneficial influence of the eccentric scholar Kumagusu Minakata.

Kumagusu Minakata

Kumagusu, who was born in Wakayama City in 1867, did not speak a word until he was six years old—but after that he never shut up. A demon for study, Kumagusu copied a 105-volume illustrated encyclopedia by hand when he was a teenager (it took him five years). When he wasn't poring over textbooks, he was in the mountains gathering insect, plant, and mineral specimens. Kumagusu also practiced Jujutsu. In 1886, he dropped out of the preparatory course for Tokyo University and headed for the United States. Kumagusu attended several schools in the United States, staying longest at State Agricultural College in Lansing, Michigan, but he rarely attended class, preferring to study on his own—again by copying nearly every book in the library and by carefully observing nature.

After leaving Lansing, Kumagusu headed to Jacksonville, Florida, to visit a well-known botanist there. In 1891, Kumagusu went to the West Indies and Central and South America to collect more botanical specimens. He also spent some time traveling with an Italian circus troupe. In 1892, Kumagusu moved to London and became a research assistant at the British Museum. Over the next eight years, Kumagusu published three hundred research papers, essays, and articles on a wide variety of subjects including botany, astronomy, anthropology, archaeology, and Oriental religions. In addition to his native Japanese, Kumagusu is reputed to have had at his command the English, French, Italian, Spanish, Portuguese, Greek, Latin, Chinese, Arabic, and Persian languages. While in London, Kumagusu relaxed by visiting Hyde Park to listen to the soap-box speakers. He also frequented neighborhood drinking establishments where he enjoyed tossing back a few pints and sampling local opinion. Kumagusu's nickname was Professor Pub. (Drinking was Kumagusu's only vice. While he admitted to having a platonic love affair with two male physicians as a young man, Kumagusu was quite proud of the fact that he never had sexual congress with another human being until he married at age forty-one. Despite his limited experience, Kumagusu wrote voluminously on the folklore and philosophy of both heterosexual and homosexual love, and he is considered to be Japan's first sexologist.)

Kumagusu corresponded with the famous Zen scholar D. T. Suzuki and made friends with the Chinese revolutionary leader Sun Yat-sen. In 1900 however, the hot-tempered Kumagusu slugged another staff member who had made a disparaging remark about the "yellow hordes of Asia." Booted out of the British Museum, Kumagusu decided to return to Japan after a sixteen-year absence.

Kumagusu settled permanently in Tanabe in 1904, where he established a kind of peoples' university, lecturing on all manner of things for the edification of the local folk. In his talks Kumagusu stressed the Mahayana/Shingon view of the world, that is, that there is a basic compatibility and interrelatedness between all peoples, East and West. The immediate issue that most concerned Kumagusu was the environment. He was well aware that runoff from the coal and copper mines being built in the Kanto Plain was polluting the rivers there, ruining the fishing and causing erosion and flooding, and he did not want that occurring in Wakayama Prefecture. Kumagusu was thus unalterably opposed to the Shrine Consolidation Policy promulgated by the national government in

1906. This was a plan to force smaller shrines, designated by the government, to merge with larger shrines. The "excess" property of the small shrines was to be confiscated and auctioned off for development. Kumagusu argued (correctly) that such a policy would result in the destruction of wildlife sanctuaries and essential watersheds, and also seriously disrupt traditional village life. Kumagusu discounted the rosy promises of Japan's capitalists—he knew that Japan's textile workers were paid even less than the native laborers of British India—and he championed the right of Tanabe farmers, fishermen, and craftspeople to earn a living wage. A protest movement was organized and Morihei enthusiastically jumped on the bandwagon, making speeches, petitioning the national government, negotiating with local authorities, and acting as Kumagusu's bodyguard.

When the government offered to build a natural history museum as a trade-off for shrine property, Kumagusu rejected the proposal with these words: "Nature has to be studied in its natural state, not in cabinets and in specimen bottles! Leave the land untouched—that is the best of all natural history museums." Following a particularly fiery denunciation of government policy Kumagusu found himself imprisoned by the authorities for a couple of weeks during the protest. He refused to be bailed out by his followers, insisting: "Why should those with money or rich friends be freed from jail while the poor have to remain locked up? Everybody should be treated the same." In the end, the Tanabe protest movement was one of the most successful in the country, and the area lost far fewer shrines than did other areas. (Even today, Kumano remains the least spoiled area of Japan; full train service was not implemented there until 1961, much later than in the rest of Japan.)

The dynamic Kumagusu—a man with an insatiable thirst for knowledge, an internationalist possessed of true vision— filled Morihei's head with the many wonders and challenges the world offered to those with the courage to seek them out.

He also taught Morihei the importance of opposing injustice and protecting the environment.

Homesteading in Hokkaido

After Morihei's first child, a daughter named Matsuko, was born in 1911, his disposition improved somewhat. When an acquaintance painted a glowing picture of the opportunities the frontier land of Hokkaido offered potential settlers, Morihei made an inspection tour to that distant northern province. Morihei met with Hokkaido's governor and made a trip around the huge island. Favorably impressed, Morihei believed that the well-watered district of Shirataki on the northern half of the island would be suitable for development, and upon his return to Tanabe he began to recruit pioneers willing to settle in the Hokkaido frontier. In a depressed economy, neither farming nor fishing held much promise for the second and third sons of families in Tanabe; many young men had already departed for Hawaii and the West Coast of the United States. Altogether, fifty-two families, composed of eighty-four people, signed up for the venture. Morihei's rich relatives put up the money for the expedition and on March 29, 1912, the group set out for their new homeland.

When the emigrants left Tanabe, cherry blossoms fluttered in the warm spring breeze; when they arrived at Kitami Ridge in Hokkaido, they were greeted by a blizzard. It took the party a month to cross the treacherous ice-caked mountain pass, and not until May 20 did they reach the intended site for their new community. Shelter, naturally, was the first priority, and by the time the buildings were up, it was too late to clear sufficient land to plant anything. They managed to cultivate the land the next year but their crop yield was poor and for the first three years the settlers subsisted on potatoes, wild vegetables, and fish caught in nearby streams. It was not an auspicious beginning for the community, and as leader of the expedition, Morihei bore the brunt of the criticism dished out by the disgruntled settlers. Keenly aware of his responsibility, Morihei worked without rest day and night to make the venture a success.

By 1915 the crops began giving better yield and the lumber business started to turn a profit. To further promote the local economy, Morihei helped develop the area's horse-breeding, pig farming, and mining industries, as well as organize the village's health, sanitation, and educational facilities. A terrible fire in 1916 destroyed eighty percent of the village (including Morihei's home) and killed three people. The disaster was a severe setback, but Morihei worked tirelessly to have everything rebuilt. Respected as a responsible and effective leader, Morihei was elected to the village council in 1917.

During the first years in Shirataki, Morihei's martial art training consisted mostly of wrestling huge logs and throwing the highwaymen who frequently ambushed him on his solitary trips. (Although Morihei dealt harshly with common criminals and escaped convicts, he was compassionate toward runaway indentured laborers—virtual slaves, lured to Hokkaido under false pretense—and ransomed or otherwise arranged for the release of dozens of these unfortunates.) Morihei was also skilled at subduing rampaging Hokkaido bears. When caught in a blizzard and snowed-in in the mountains, Morihei would share his provisions with the massive beasts, and it is said that the bears would see him down off the mountain when the snow lifted and he returned to the village.

During his years in Hokkaido, Morihei, then in his vigorous thirties, was obsessed with physical power and endurance. He single-handedly felled five hundred trees a year with a specially made ax that weighed three times more than average. He uprooted stumps with his bare hands, broke thick branches across his back, and played tug-of-war with draft horses. When a horse-and-buggy rig fell into a ravine,

Morihei was summoned to haul it out, driver, contents, and all, with one mighty heave. On horseback he had to exercise caution when he squeezed the stirrups to avoid breaking the horse's ribs. He performed his meditations outdoors and continued his daily practice of dousing himself with ice-cold water, no mean feat in frigid Hokkaido winters. Morihei evidently taught himself to generate internal heat, similar to Tibetan "sky-clad" hermits who can defrost frozen towels placed on their bare skin. Morihei later told his disciples that the spot where he purified himself did not freeze over even during the coldest part of the year.

On a lighter note, Morihei had a brief (and totally uncharacteristic) love affair with a young girl from Tanabe during the early days in Hokkaido. The affair came to an abrupt end with the arrival of Mrs. Ueshiba, who had been left behind in Wakayama until proper accommodations were built in Shirataki.

The most momentous event of Morihei's sojourn in Hokkaido was his encounter with Sokaku Takeda (1859–1943), the dreaded grand master of Daito Ryu Jujutsu.

Sokaku Takeda

Sokaku, the last of the old-time warriors, was born in Aizu (present-day Fukushima Prefecture). In a country of fierce samurai, Aizu warriors were feared as the fiercest. As soon as Sokaku could walk he was taught swordsmanship, spear fighting, combat Jujutsu, and Sumo by his exceedingly severe grandfather and father—if the boy failed to master a technique quickly enough he had his fingers singed. Sokaku bore the scars with pride, however, and all he cared about were the fighting arts. He ignored book studies completely and never learned to read or write. "Don't worry, I'll get people to read and write for me," he assured his father when Sokaku was warned of the potential perils of illiteracy.

The die-hard Aizu warriors were among the last to capitulate to the imperial forces during the civil war of 1868 and if Sokaku had been a little older he would have been compelled to commit *seppuku* (ritual suicide by slicing open the belly) with the famous Byakko-Tai ("Aizu's Boys' Army"). For Sokaku, the battles waged near his ancestral home were edifying, albeit bloody, entertainment; he hid in the bushes picking up pointers on the best methods of dispatching opponents.

The Aizu clan was finally defeated, and after his mother died when he was thirteen, the young Sokaku took off on an old-fashioned warrior's pilgrimage, first apprenticing himself to master martial artists and then challenging all comers everywhere he went, from Okinawa in the south to Hokkaido in the north. Sokaku spent his youth as a street fighter, engaging in scores of no-holds-barred fights to the finish, killing a number of opponents. In 1882, Sokaku got into an argument with a gang of construction workers in Fukushima; he drew his sword when they attacked him with pick axes, iron rods, and bricks. Sokaku slashed his way through the crowd, leaving behind many dead and wounded. He was arrested and charged with manslaughter but later released after it was judged that he had acted in self-defense. The authorities confiscated his sword, however, and warned him to behave himself. The judge told him, "The age of the samurai warrior is over."

In 1875 Sokaku was summoned back to Aizu to assume a hereditary position of Shinto priest. He was to be instructed by the distinguished scholar/martial artist/priest Saigo Tanomo (also known as Chikanori Hoshina). Tanomo was also the only remaining elder of the Aizu clan capable of imparting the secret *oshiki-uchi* techniques.

It unclear exactly what the oshiki-uchi techniques encompassed. Some researchers believe that the oshiki-uchi techniques mostly emphasized samurai etiquette (the literal meaning of oshiki-uchi is "within the lord's castle") and that Tanomo was not a martial artist at all. However, Sokaku kept a number of impressive scrolls (which he could not read) cataloguing martial art techniques in great detail and tracing the lineage of the oshiki-uchi system back to the emperor Minamoto (Genji) Yoshimitsu who lived in the twelfth century—Sokaku himself was listed as thirty-fifth grand master of the tradition—and it is likely that these elaborate documents came from Tanomo. At any rate, Sokaku began teaching a system, which he called "Yamato" and then "Daito" Ryu. The Daito Ryu system was a combination of classical Jujutsu and practical fighting techniques based on Sokaku's unsurpassed experience in hand-to-hand combat and his facility with deadly weapons. (Incidentally, the weapon Sokaku feared as the most difficult to defend against was the *kusarigama,* sickle and chain.)

Sokaku was obviously not cut out to be a Shinto priest, so he relied on his exceptional prowess in the martial arts to provide his livelihood. Around 1888 the thirty-year-old Sokaku began establishing himself as the premier martial art instructor of the time. Sokaku was tiny, less than five feet tall, and thin. Nonetheless, he made short work of each and every challenger. His extraordinary ability was due to mind control, technical perfection honed in countless battles, and mastery of *aiki,* the blending of positive and negative energy. Although he never learned to read a book, Sokaku could read men's minds. Prior to offering instruction, Sokaku would survey the prospective students, often dismissing several, seemingly at random and for no apparent reason. When questioned about this later, Sokaku would respond, for example, "The first one is a drunkard, the second one is a womanizer, and the third is a troublemaker. I don't teach such people." Sokaku's intuitions were invariably right on the mark.

In an attempt to lead a more normal life, Sokaku married

and built a house; however, his wife died while giving birth to their second child and a fire destroyed his home shortly thereafter. Sokaku subsequently placed his children with relatives and once again assumed a wandering life, where he lived on the fringes of society.

Between 1898 and 1915, when Morihei met him in Hokkaido, Sokaku traveled from place to place, mostly in northern Japan, making a living by conducting seminars. In 1904 Charles Parry, a British citizen teaching English at the Sendai Higher School, disliked the looks of a strangely dressed Japanese passenger sharing his first-class compartment and asked the conductor to check the fellow's ticket. (Sokaku decked himself out in slightly shabby Japanese clothes, tall wooden sandals, a big bowler-type hat, a walking stick—with a razor-sharp blade concealed in the tip—and a large cloth bag containing his teaching licenses and registry book.) When Sokaku demanded to know why he alone was being asked to show his ticket the conductor informed him of the foreign gentleman's complaint. The enraged Sokaku jumped out of his seat and rushed over to Parry for an explanation. Parry leapt up, confident that his six-foot height would intimidate the diminutive Sokaku. Instead, Sokaku swiftly grabbed Parry's brandished fists, applied an excruciating pressure-point hold, and then tossed Parry through the air to the back of the compartment. After recovering from the shock of the throw, Parry humbly apologized and asked to be accepted as a student, becoming Sokaku's first foreign disciple. (The total number of people listed as receiving instruction in Sokaku's registry books is reported to exceed thirty thousand.)

Around 1911, Sokaku was invited by the police bureau in Hokkaido to train its officers. In addition to legitimate settlers, such as Morihei's group from Tanabe, the wide-open frontier of Hokkaido was a haven for brigands—pirates infested the coast and highwaymen roamed the interior. Gangs, prototypes of today's *yakuza*, ran smuggling, gambling, and slave labor operations. Police were largely powerless and out-numbered; in fact several stations had been sacked by the gangs.

Much like a United States marshal called in to restore law and order to a wild cow town, Sokaku, then in his fifties, made his way to the untamed wilderness. Gangsters, alerted to Sokaku's arrival, immediately put a tail on the tiny warrior. When they discovered that he visited a public bath every morning, unarmed, six hooligans were assigned to teach him a thing or two about Hokkaido gangster manners. Sokaku was unfazed by the attack. The snap of a wet towel can raise welts on bare flesh even in the hands of a schoolboy. When Sokaku projected his *ki* into the makeshift weapon, he knocked the thugs senseless or cracked their ribs. Terrified by Sokaku's fearsome ability, a small army of thugs surrounded Sokaku's hotel and clamored for a showdown. The defiant Sokaku obtained a sword and vowed to strew the streets with dead bodies, and the town's citizens scrambled for cover. In the best tradition of a Hollywood western, a truce was arranged between the gang leader and Sokaku and bloodshed was avoided.

Sokaku paid a high price for obtaining such a fearsome reputation. Enemies—the family, friends, disciples, and henchmen of people he had cut down—were everywhere, and Sokaku stayed constantly on the move to foil his pursuers. He would never enter any building, even his own residence, without calling out first to make someone he knew come out to greet him and escort him inside. Once Sokaku and Morihei were playing a game of go at Morihei's residence when one of Morihei's neighbors came in. The neighbor's face was partially obscured by a large scarf and Sokaku grabbed the heavy go board and began beating the man over the head, knocking him silly before Morihei could intervene. Sokaku simply mumbled, "I thought it was one of my enemies out to get me." Sokaku would not take any food or drink unless it was tested by one of his students first, lest it be poisoned. No one (except his wife) was allowed to come within three feet of him. He slept with a dagger and an iron fan and shifted his bed several times a night to confuse would-be attackers. When he did sleep he often cried out in terror, haunted by the faces of the men he had slain.

On a trip to Engaru in February of 1915 Morihei learned that Sokaku was conducting a session at a nearby inn and immediately rushed to attend. After witnessing an impressive demonstration and being handled deftly by the skinny Sokaku, Morihei asked to be accepted as a Daito Ryu student. Forgetting about everything else, Morihei stayed at the inn for a month. Thereafter, Morihei trained with Sokaku at every opportunity he had, building a dojo on his property and inviting Sokaku to stay with him. Morihei received private instruction from Sokaku for two hours most mornings, and attended the demanding master from morning to night, personally preparing Sokaku's meals, washing his clothes, massaging his shoulders, and assisting him in the bath.

On occasion, Sokaku used Morihei as a stand-in to deal with some of the death threats he was constantly receiving, figuring, no doubt, that such practical hands-on experience would benefit his star student. Thus, Morihei was forced to square off against opponents who were intent on killing him. Details are sketchy but it appears that Morihei never responded in kind, and subdued the attackers without fatal results.

Following the great fire in 1916 Morihei had less time to train with Sokaku, although he did continue to accompany him on occasional instruction tours to various parts of Hokkaido.

Morihei and his family (which now included a son, Takemori, born in 1917) suddenly left Hokkaido for good at the end of 1919. Word had arrived informing him of his father's grave illness back in Tanabe (Yoroku had actually lived with his son in Shirataki for a time but couldn't bear the cold), and it appears that his infatuation with Sokaku was coming to an end. Whatever the reason, Morihei unhesitatingly abandoned everything he owned in Shirataki, turning over the bulk of his possessions to Sokaku (who had married a much younger woman who eventually bore him seven children). Thirty-six-year-old Morihei did not rush straight back to Tanabe, however; he made a detour to Ayabe, a small town near Kyoto, where he had yet another fateful encounter, this time with one of the most enigmatic figures of the twentieth century, Onisaburo Deguchi.

Omoto-kyo and Onisaburo Deguchi

As the old order disintegrated in nineteenth-century Japan, there was a surge of hope that a new age would emerge from the chaos. Suddenly there were seers, prophets, and messiahs everywhere, each one promising liberation from the fighting, disease, and hardship then engulfing their world.

Many of the founders of these new religious movements were women. Indeed, during this tumultuous period it was pure-hearted women who came forth to be mouthpieces of the gods—not aristocratic ladies sheltered from the harsh realities of life, but simple, desperately poor peasant women who demanded redress and reform.

One of the most prominent of these prophetesses was Nao Deguchi, founder of Omoto-kyo. Born in 1836 to an impoverished family during one of the worst famines in Japan's history, Nao miraculously escaped "thinning out"—the euphemism for infanticide, which was typically aimed at female newborns. Tens of thousands of people starved to death in the Great Tempo Famine. For several consecutive years the crops failed—every blade of grass, every root and piece of grain, all the leaves and bark of trees, even old tatami mats were devoured by the famished hordes. Although Nao survived this disaster, the rest of her life was one long, unrelenting ordeal. She recalled later in life, "I cannot remember ever having a full stomach."

When she was ten years old, Nao's alcoholic father died and the young girl was sent out to work, slaving away as a maid, shop girl, and seamstress to help support her family. At seventeen, Nao was adopted into the Deguchi family by her aunt, a sullen lady who committed suicide two years later. Nao's first engagement was broken off by her relatives and, at age twenty, she was betrothed to a man she did not love.

Since her new husband was a master carpenter, among the highest-paid craftsmen of the time, there was a glimmer of hope that Nao's fortune would improve. Sadly, her easygoing husband was addicted to sake and vaudeville; the combination of heavy drinking, late nights on the town, and injuries suffered on jobs took their toll, and eventually the hapless fellow became an unemployed invalid. Instead of prospering, Nao's family fell deeper and deeper into debt, eventually losing everything they owned.

Of the eleven children Nao bore between the ages of twenty and forty-seven, three died at birth, two went insane, one was killed in the Sino-Japanese War, one attempted suicide, and three ran away from home. After her husband's death when she was fifty-one years old, Nao was reduced to rag-picking to eke out the meagerest of livings.

From her youth, Nao frequently heard inner voices and she came under the influence of the Konko-kyo religion founded by the peasant Bunjiro Kawate in 1859. Kawate believed himself to be the incarnation of Tenchi-Kane-no-Kami (also known as Ushitora-no-Konjin, or simply Konjin); this previously obscure deity, once considered a wrathful *kami* of minor significance, was actually, Kawate claimed, the supreme god of love that would lead humankind into a golden age of peace and prosperity. The god's message, as interpreted by Kawate, was, "Reform the world, heal the sick, and prepare for a new era."

In 1892 the fifty-seven-year-old Nao received a personal

summons from that august deity. One night, Nao suddenly felt as if she were drifting among the clouds, her body as light and transparent as a feather; her wretched little room was filled with soft light and a lovely fragrance. "I am Konjin," she heard a masculine voice from deep within her exclaim. At Konjin's direction, Nao neither slept nor ate for the next thirteen days as she continually purified herself with cold water ablutions in order to prepare herself for further instructions from the great god.

At the behest of her god, Nao sold what little she had and became a beggar. Shaking violently, uttering strange guttural sounds, and crying out the prophetic utterances of Konjin in a loud and lordly manner, Nao began attracting attention, some of it unwanted. After mumbling something about the world being purified by fire, the police suspected her of being the arsonist then terrorizing the neighborhood. She was taken into custody and only released when the real arsonist confessed. Following this incident, Konjin ordered the illiterate Nao to take dictation. Writing "automatically" in simple *kana* script, Nao eventually filled some 100,000 pages with notes called *Fudesaki* ("Writings"). Her basic theme: "The time is come and the world needs to be completely cleansed and reformed! Emperors, kings, and all forms of artificial government must be done away with, and true equality established; abolish capitalism, return to the land, and do not let the selfish and greedy prosper at the expense of the righteous and diligent. Wake up and heed the call of Konjin!"

News of Nao's clairvoyance and ability to heal illness spread and a small group of devoted followers gathered around her in Ayabe. Her initial group was under the umbrella of the Konko-kyo organization, but eventually Nao established her own religion, which she called Omoto-kyo.

In 1898 Nao was approached by a dapper young man named Kisaburo Ueda. Born near Kameoka in 1871, Ueda also came from a family that had fallen on hard times. (Later, Ueda claimed that he was actually the illegitimate son of an imperial prince.) Ueda's grandfather had gambled away most of the family's once-considerable holdings, and the household was desperately poor. Ueda was largely raised by his grandmother, an unusually well-educated woman for that period. She was a skilled poet and a keen student of the sacred science of *kototama* (sound-spirit), having learned the subject from her father, the top expert of his day.

The boy's weak constitution and frequent illnesses delayed his entrance into school for three years, but his brilliance allowed him to catch up quickly and then to surpass all the others. Unfortunately, his classmates, and even a teacher—who did not care to be corrected by one of his pupils—were jealous of Ueda's genius and cruelly teased and mistreated the young scholar. The tables were turned when Ueda was appointed assistant instructor at the tender age of twelve; however, the outspoken youth had difficulty getting along with his much older colleagues and consequently resigned his position two years later.

Ueda returned home, working as a farmer, peddler, and day laborer to support himself. He was a tireless autodidact, much like Kumagusu. At night, he continued his study of literature and practiced calligraphy (after some practice, he could write sixty Chinese characters a minute, an incredible rate) and painting (Ueda was related to the famous artist Okyo Maruyama and soon displayed a similar genius). From the age of eighteen, Ueda began contributing verse and essays to literary journals. He sometimes wrote under a female pseudonym and his poetry was unquestioningly accepted for publication by many women's magazines. Ueda was particularly good at *kyoka*, satirical "mad verse."

In his early twenties, Ueda familiarized himself with folk medicine and studied veterinary science (carefully dissecting various kinds of animals before eating them). Dairy science was one of his specialties, which he knew well enough to start up a milk-products business. Ueda learned the language of beasts, enabling him to calm spooked horses or coax stubborn oxen into more work by speaking to them in a soft voice. He expanded his liberal arts education by learning classical Japanese music and dance. Ueda was never an ivory tower scholar; right from the start of his career he was a community activist, not hesitant to oppose village elders if he felt there had been an injustice. To some Ueda was a champion of the poor and oppressed; to others he was a meddlesome troublemaker disturbing the status quo. Argumentative and a bit of a dandy, Ueda was a favorite target of the local toughs and he was attacked and brutally beaten more than once.

In 1897 Ueda lost his father and underwent a spiritual crisis. Depressed, harassed by bullies, involved with prostitutes, and drinking heavily, the twenty-eight-year-old ran from the village and sequestered himself in a cave on Mount Takakusa, determined to find the truth or perish in the attempt.

There, during a week-long fast, Ueda entered, he claimed, a divine trance and toured the cosmos: angels accompanied him back to the dawn of creation and then far into the future revealing the ultimate destiny of humankind; gods and buddhas taught the flighty young mystic all their secrets. Thus enlightened and claiming clairvoyance and clairaudience, Ueda descended the mountain ready to devote himself to the salvation of the world.

At first, Ueda did not get much of a response to his preaching about the mysteries of existence. He was dismissed as just another demented prophet by the villagers and even his own family was embarrassed by Ueda's ranting. His resolutely dissolute brothers repeatedly smashed his altars and hurled stones at him when he tried to do purification rites in the river. The police got after him for "proselytizing without a license." Under pressure from the authorities, Ueda decided to establish his credentials.

Ueda initially studied with the noted spiritualist Otate Nagasawa, who was then a teacher on Mount Ontake, home of one of Japan's foremost mountain religions. Nagasawa was the main disciple of Shintoku Honda, the charismatic leader responsible for the revival of the ancient *chinkon-kishin* ("calm the spirit and return to the divine") Shinto meditation technique. Following several months of intense study with Nagasawa, Ueda was given permission to act as a *saniwa,* a kind of psychic umpire who decided cases of spirit possession.

One day, while performing rites at a shrine, Ueda heard a voice telling him to go to the west because someone was awaiting his arrival there. Ueda immediately set out in that direction even though he had no idea whom he was supposed to meet. As he was sitting in a tea shop, the proprietress asked him his business.

"I'm a saniwa," Ueda announced.

"Oh, how fortunate!" the woman exclaimed. "My mother is a mouthpiece for the god Konjin, and she has told us she is expecting a divine messenger from the east. We opened this tea shop to search for the messenger, hoping that he would stop here. By all means, you must be introduced to her."

It is impossible to imagine two people more unlike than Nao Deguchi and Kisaburo Ueda. Tiny old Nao was re-served, abstemious, and guileless; she neither cut nor combed her hair and she rejected silk, tobacco, animal food, and Western clothes and customs. Ueda was outgoing, full of gusto, and shrewd; he was a *bon vivant* who designed his own fantastic garments, favoring such material as bright red crepe. Nao, a simple, frugal woman, shied away from the limelight; Ueda, a flamboyant polymath-artist-entrepreneur, craved it. Interestingly, in subsequent Omoto-kyo hagiography, Nao is described as "a man's spirit in a woman's body," while Ueda is thought of as "a woman's spirit in a man's body" (who later on enjoyed appearing in full drag).

Despite the dramatic circumstances of their first encounter, it took both sides some time to conclude that the other party was the genuine article. After several months of wary negoti-ation, Nao and Ueda agreed to combine forces. Ueda moved to Ayabe, married Nao's sixteen-year-old daughter Sumi (born when her mother was forty-seven), and adopted the

name Onisaburo (also read Wanisaburo) Deguchi. Onisaburo and Sumi had eight children: two sons died in infancy,
one daughter died when she was sixteen, and the five remaining daughters all adopted husbands into the Deguchi clan.

Not long after joining the Deguchi family, Onisaburo attempted a takeover of the movement. He had big plans, but
he ran into opposition from Nao's inner circle and then from
Nao herself, who complained bitterly about his bewildering
innovations (including the "editing" of Nao's divinely inspired missives). Onisaburo considered Nao's views too extreme. She denounced schools, education, and *kanji* (Chinese
characters) as "great evils," and she refused to have her
grandchildren vaccinated—despite a heavy fine and the threat
of arrest from public health officials—because the vaccine
came from an animal and had been developed in a foreign
country. (Onisaburo secretly paid the fine for her.) Nao also
mistakenly predicted that Japan would suffer a crushing defeat in the Russo-Japanese War, damaging the group's credi-
bility. In spite of a series of troubles—Nao's flight to a cave in
protest, Onisaburo's temporary expulsion from the movement, rumor of assassination plots against him, lack of funds,
and so on—Onisaburo's leadership prevailed. Nao died in
1918 at the age of eighty-two. Reportedly in deep depression,
her final words were, "Pity the poor workers! Pity the poor
soldiers!" Following Nao's death, Onisaburo, the "Holy
Guru," assumed total control of the movement. Titular leadership of Omoto-kyo passed to Sumi Deguchi, Nao's daughter and Onisaburo's wife.

Onisaburo was definitely on a different plane from that of
the other simple-minded religious cranks, deluded messiahs,
and clever frauds that populated that era. In addition to pos-
sessing a brilliant mind, Onisaburo was an artist par excel-
lence. His literary output is likely unequaled by anyone: he
dictated over 600,000 poems and a number of books, including the incredible eighty-one-volume *Reiki Monogatari* (*Tales
of the Spiritual World*). In this stupendous work—its outline

alone runs to over four hundred pages—Onisaburo roams the cosmos interpreting past, present, and future events in terms of kototama theory, as well as giving advice on more mundane matters such as the proper height of one's bed ("less than three feet high, unless you are the emperor"); personal hygiene ("men do not have an absolute right to enter the bath before women; it depends who is dirtier"); and marriage ("couples should not be too much in love; otherwise they defer to each other, constantly avoiding the hard decisions necessary to maintain a household").

(Much of the material in the *Reiki Monogatari* is reminiscent of the writings of the eighteenth-century Swedish mystic Emmanuel Swedenborg. At age fifty-five the genius scientist and inventor—among whose papers were discovered detailed plans for airplanes and submarines—had a vision of Christ and he spent the next twenty-seven years on guided tours of the cosmos. It is said that Swedenborg spent half of his time here on earth as a hardheaded scientist and half of his time in heaven, speaking with angels and other spirits. In his diaries Swedenborg also reported having sex with divine maidens. Onisaburo was familiar with Swedenborg's ideas because several of Swedenborg's books had been translated into Japanese by D. T. Suzuki early in the century.)

Onisaburo loved music and he composed religious anthems, folk songs, love ballads, even waltzes and tangos. He also tried his hand at play writing, composing, movie directing, and sculpture, but he truly excelled at calligraphy, painting, and pottery. Regardless of what one thinks of his ideas, Onisaburo was undoubtedly one of East Asia's most gifted visual artists. His splendid free-flowing brushwork brought his characters and images to life and his dramatic, brightly colored ceramics are rightly considered to rank as "national treasures."

Onisaburo was an effective spiritual teacher, soothing thousands with his chinkon-kishin meditation techniques. Nao and her early followers engaged in a frantic type of spirit possession, accompanied by wild gestures and punctuated with loud cries. Onisaburo preferred a quieter, more meditative form of communication with the gods. "Prayer should be natural and to the point," he taught. His prophecies were ambiguous enough to allow him to boast of a nearly perfect batting average. Some of his prophecies were right on the money: "Someday in Japan temple bells and Buddha images will be melted down and turned into armaments, children of fifteen will be called up to be killed in battle, and everyone will suffer terribly." These events are exactly what occurred later on during World War II. He was, like many similar charismatic figures, good at curing psychosomatic illnesses. A master psychologist, Onisaburo was a skilled "mind-reader," sufficiently clairvoyant to disarm skeptics by, for example, telling them exactly how much money they had in their pockets.

Unshakably optimistic, Onisaburo good-humoredly survived a series of setbacks that would have crushed the spirit of an ordinary mortal. Onisaburo confided to his followers that during his seven-day trance on Mount Takakusa he had been "killed, split in two, dashed to pieces, frozen solid, burnt to ashes, and buried alive." Compared to those experiences in the spiritual world, nothing here on earth could faze him. He thought of himself as the modern version of the Shinto god Susano-o-no-mikoto, the mischievous deity forever in trouble because of his antics.

All of this, coupled with his majestic appearance—surrounded by a bevy of beautiful women, clad in a resplendent kimono with a colorful shaman's hat over his piled-up mane of hair—made Onisaburo an indeed impressive, often irresistible leader. For the first time, a new religion began to attract intellectuals, aristocrats, government officials, and military men, rather than merely disgruntled farmers and innocent country folk. One of Onisaburo's first and most important converts was the famed professor of English, Wasaburo Asano, translator of Shakespeare's works into

Japanese. Attracting people of that caliber helped the cult boom: between 1919 and 1921, the "Golden Age of Omoto-kyo," membership reached several million people, and millions more were directly influenced by Omoto-kyo publications, including a daily newspaper.

Even in remote Hokkaido, word of the exciting new religion headquartered in Ayabe reached Morihei's ears. When Morihei departed from Shirataki he was not drawn to Tanabe but to Ayabe, where he came face to face with the Holy Guru himself.

As soon as Morihei stepped off the train at Ayabe station, he sensed something different—the entire area percolated with energy. The spectacle at the majestic Omoto-kyo headquarters took Morihei's breath away. Scores of long-haired men and women, clad in bright kimonos and flowing skirts, bustled around huge halls and sacred ponds, resolved to "reform the world and create heaven on earth." Overwhelmed, Morihei found himself drawn toward the Dragon Pavilion. There he took a seat in a dimly lit corner and began softly reciting the Shingon chants and prayers he had years before committed to memory. Suddenly, an apparition of his father appeared before him. Then another figure emerged from the darkness, saying, "What do you see?"

"My father," Morihei replied sadly. "He looks so old and wasted away."

"Your father is fine," Onisaburo gently said to Morihei. "Let him go."

Completely enthralled with the otherworldly air of Ayabe, Morihei lingered on for several more days, speaking to Onisaburo, learning about Omoto-kyo doctrine, and joining chinkon-kishin meditation sessions.

When he finally returned to Tanabe, Morihei was shocked to find that his father had, as Onisaburo hinted, passed away peacefully. Morihei was informed of his father's last words to his temperamental yet beloved son: "Let nothing bind you— live the way you want."

Morihei and Omoto-kyo

For the next few months, Morihei behaved as if mad. He spoke to no one and passed each night alone in the mountains furiously swinging his sword. Then, to everyone's consternation, he unexpectedly announced his intention to move to Ayabe and join Omoto-kyo. His family and friends were aghast at the plan—Omoto-kyo had recently received a lot of bad press, and, as his wife complained, "Why leave this place when we have productive land and fine neighbors? Are the gods there that you say are calling you going to pay you a salary?"

Once Morihei's mind was made up, however, there was no turning back. In the spring of 1920, the thirty-seven-year-old Morihei, his wife and two children, and his mother made the move to Ayabe. (Morihei purchased, just before the move, a three-year supply of rice as a kind of insurance policy.)

After settling in a small house near the main shrine, Morihei assisted with Omoto-kyo's many farming and construction projects then in full swing and participated in the various prayer services, meditation sessions, special fasts, and purification ceremonies with the community. He threw himself into the study of Omoto-kyo creeds and, after being taught by Onisaburo that art is the mother of religion, took up calligraphy and poetry composition.

The people of Omoto-kyo regarded agriculture as the basis of the new world order and stressed natural farming methods and wholesome food. Animals were not kept at Ayabe, and since the use of human "night soil" was inappropriate for vegetables offered in the shrines, Omoto-kyo organic farmers developed a highly refined system of composting.

Throughout his life, Morihei was passionately fond of farming. With the abolition of feudalism, many former samurai rediscovered the affinity between Budo and farming, two disciplines that promoted clean living and high thoughts. Morihei had extra-heavy tools forged for him and wielded his hoe with the same concentration and extension as he did his sword.

Morihei was in charge of composting and rose each day at three o'clock in the morning to collect waste material from a number of far-flung places. One day he cleared a field of kudzu and dragged an enormous clump of vines back along the road to Ayabe. On the way, a pedestrian accidentally got tangled in the vines, and Morihei, single-mindedly going full blast, covered another mile before finally hearing the poor fellow's cry for help.

Initially, Morihei practiced martial arts by himself in the evenings. After an Omoto-kyo fire brigade was organized, he directed the training drills, which included basic martial art techniques. Onisaburo requested that Morihei teach martial arts to the other Omoto-kyo believers, partly for character building and partly to train a group of bodyguards. A building was remodeled to house the Ueshiba Academy, Morihei's first dojo.

Onisaburo's daughter Naohi, who later became head of Omoto-kyo, was one of Morihei's earliest students. She recalled, "He made no allowances for women trainees, and treated male and female the same during practice. It was hard on us girls, but we appreciated not being made to feel inferior because of our sex." While Morihei taught mostly practical self-defense to his students, he continued to research sword and spear movements on his own.

The opening of Morihei's first training hall in 1920 was the only happy event of Morihei's first year in Ayabe. During that year Morihei's two sons, Takemori (age three), born in Hokkaido, and Kuniharu (age six months), born in Ayabe, died of illness within three weeks of each other. And on February 11, 1921, the First Omoto-kyo Incident occurred.

For several years, the government had been monitoring Omoto-kyo activities with increasing suspicion and alarm.

Nao had been virulently opposed to the emperor system, but Onisaburo was more tactful, composing clever poems that seemed to pay lip service to the imperial system (while actually ridiculing it) and keeping company with high-profile nationalists. (In true form, Onisaburo secretly associated with left-wing radicals as well, going so far as to shield some of them from government prosecution by hiding them on the Omoto-kyo compound.) His pacifist and anticapitalist views were of additional concern to the warmongers in the government. Onisaburo wrote in 1895 after the Sino-Japanese War, "The real fight is not against foreign adversaries but against those here at home who suppress our freedom, trample on our human rights, crush peace, and destroy our culture for the sake of profit." Overenthusiastic Omoto-kyo followers were spreading rumors that both Nao and Onisaburo had prophesied that there would be a war between Japan and the rest of the world in the not-too-distant future and that Japanese society would be reformed from top to bottom. The true emperor of Japan was not the sickly Taisho occupying the palace in Tokyo but the dynamic spiritual leader residing in Ayabe. A new order would emerge, and Onisaburo was the one destined to establish a universal kingdom of peace, love, and brotherhood.

Other more vicious rumors were spread by Onisaburo's enemies: Nao's tomb was as regal as that of an empress and Onisaburo's residence was modeled after the imperial palace; weapons, explosives, food, and money were stockpiled on the Omoto-kyo compound; Omoto-kyo followers were weaving an enormous battle flag to rally behind when the revolution was launched; secret caves and tunnels were filled with sex slaves used to breed more Omoto-kyo members and hide the bodies of those who dared to cross Onisaburo and his minions.

Sufficiently alarmed, authorities raided the Omoto-kyo headquarters. No weapons or bodies were discovered but Onisaburo and several of his chief aides were arrested on trumped-up charges of lese majesty and violation of the

Newspaper Control Act. Onisaburo was quickly convicted and given a five-year sentence. The government also had the main Omoto-kyo buildings destroyed. Onisaburo's conviction (he was subsequently released on bail while the sentence was appealed) and the destruction of Omoto-kyo put a damper on things at Ayabe for the next two years. In that period, Morihei quietly devoted himself to farming, study, and martial art training. Kisshomaru, Morihei's final child and sole surviving son, was born in June 1921. Morihei's mother, Yuki, died in early 1922.

At the end of April in 1922, Sokaku turned up in Ayabe with his wife and ten-year-old son. It is a matter of contention whether or not Sokaku invited himself to Ayabe or if he was asked to come and instruct by Morihei. At any rate, Onisaburo took an immediate dislike to the cocky little brawler— "The man reeks of blood and violence"—and Sokaku made no effort to conceal his contempt for Omoto-kyo. After a very tense six-month stay, Sokaku was persuaded to leave Ayabe. Sokaku visited Morihei a few times after this, but Morihei was already well along a much different path from that of the Daito Ryu grand master, and by 1936 Morihei refused to meet with Sokaku. (Sokaku continued his itinerant existence until his death in 1943, at the age of eighty-four.)

Onisaburo was called many things during his eventful career, ranging from "Savior of the World" to "The Biggest Charlatan in History." A childhood acquaintance once said of Onisaburo, "It was impossible to tell if he was an absolute genius or a complete fool," and he remained an enigma until the day he died. Perhaps the title most apt was "The Ultimate Don Quixote." One of his favorite poems was

> Form the sun, earth,
> And moon
> Into a sweet cake,
> Cover it with stardust,
> And swallow it whole!

Onisaburo was further convinced that he was the incarnation of Miroku, the Buddha scheduled to appear and usher in a golden age of peace and prosperity. It was this heartfelt belief in his destiny that led Onisaburo to undertake the Great Mongolian Adventure.

The Great Mongolian Adventure

The goal of Japanese nationalists was the creation of a Greater East Asian Coprosperity Sphere, with the rest of the world being divided between the Europeans and the Americans. They particularly had their eyes on the vast, underpopulated, underdeveloped, but resource-rich plains of Manchuria and Mongolia. The people there were miserably poor, ignorant, and dominated by evil Buddhist lamas; Japan would magnanimously liberate the area from Chinese control, assist Mongolian patriots in creating an independent nation, and kindly advise their brothers and sisters on the "proper" way to run a country.

To that end, countless Japanese secret societies and spy rings were operating in Northeast Asia. The largest and most notorious of these groups was the Black Dragon Society (or more correctly, the Amur River Society), founded by the right-wing activist and martial artist Ryohei Ueda in 1901. Membership ranged from cabinet ministers and senior military officers to agents provocateurs, spies, and hired assassins.

In stark contrast to Europeans and Americans, who barely tolerated the disreputable business of spying and espionage as a necessary evil, nearly every Japanese citizen regarded intelligence gathering and counterespionage as highly patriotic acts to be proud of. The incredible dedication of the large number of high-ranking military officers, many of them from aristocratic families, who were willing to labor away for years posing as coolies, longshoremen, houseboys, cooks, hotel keepers, female and male prostitutes, Jujutsu instructors, Buddhist monks, converts to Islam and Russian Orthodox Christianity, and so on simply to acquire scraps of information is beyond the comprehension of Westerners. One Western intelligence officer operating in Manchuria during this period wrote in his memoirs that it was usually impossible to judge the race, rank, or age within twenty years of a Japanese spy. Or even his sex. A captain of the Imperial Army, disguised as a woman, worked as a cook for a foreign diplomat five years before being found out (much to the regret of the diplomat's family: "She was the best cook we ever had"). Every Japanese in China was, in effect, a spy passing along whatever he or she had seen.

Shadowy Yutaro Yano, a retired naval commander and active gunrunner with links to the Black Dragon Society, invited Onisaburo to Mongolia, optimistic that the charismatic religious leader would win the people's confidence, thus paving the way for a smooth takeover by Japanese-supported Mongolian warlords. (Yano later turned against Onisaburo and advocated the destruction of Omoto-kyo. He was imprisoned by the government for some reason and died in jail, rumored to have been poisoned.)

For years, Onisaburo dreamed of becoming the spiritual and temporal leader of not just little Japan but the entire world. To facilitate communication between the far-flung branches of his future kingdom, Onisaburo enthusiastically promoted Esperanto and romanized Japanese as universal languages. Onisaburo made contacts with like-minded groups overseas (such as people of the Baha'i faith) that advocated the synthesis of world religions and the creation of an international government. Onisaburo shared the belief of Swedenborg that a new Jerusalem was due to descend to earth. When Yano's invitation arrived Onisaburo interpreted it as a divine summons to fashion heaven on earth: China, Manchuria, Mongolia, Tibet, Siberia, Russia, and India would be forged into the paradise of Shambhala. (Sweden-

borg had written of a "Great Tartary" in the East but if Onisaburo had lived in the West he may have gone to Chicago to
look for Shambhala. In 1909, the architect Daniel Burnham,
chief designer of the widely praised White City that served as
the venue for the 1893 World's Fair, submitted a detailed
master plan for Chicago, largely based on details of the heavenly city described by Swedenborg in his book *Heaven and
Its Wonders and Hell*.)

The supremely confident Onisaburo surreptitiously departed for the Chinese mainland in early February of 1924. Accompanying him were the lawyer Matsumura (a world
government would need an attorney general right away to
draw up a suitable legal code), the English-speaking barber
Nada (the savior of the world must be presentable at all times
and required an interpreter to speak to his subjects in the
West), the bodyguard *extraordinaire* Morihei (future commander of the international army), and the impresario Yano. The
small party inconspicuously made their way through Korea, at
that time under Japanese occupation, and then to Fengtian
(present-day Shenyang). There they were met by several Black
Dragon Society agents to act as guide-interpreters.

The situation in that corner of Asia was chaotic. The fledg-
ling Chinese republic, only twelve years in existence, was engaged in running battles with regional warlords and bandit
chiefs for control of the area. Japanese troops stationed
nearby were eagerly awaiting any pretense they could use to
invade Manchuria and the Soviet Red Army was poised on
the border of Outer Mongolia looking for similar opportunities. Manchuria was swarming with spies and espionage
agents working on behalf of a score of competing domestic
and foreign interests, and overrun with adventurers, corrupt
traders, con artists, and assorted riffraff.

Yano was in cahoots with a Mongolian bandit chief known
as Lu Chan-kuei, the Tiger of Manchuria. He urged Lu to
form a coalition with Chang Tso-lin, the dominant warlord
in the area, and to rebel against the Chinese central govern-

ment, demanding the establishment of an independent Manchurian-Mongolian state. (Chang was assassinated later in June of 1928 by the Japanese Kwantung Army, the event that precipitated war in Asia.) "We will help you secure materiel," Yano assured Lu, "and with the services of Onisaburo you will capture people's hearts."

A meeting was arranged between Lu and Onisaburo and subsequently it was agreed that the Omoto-kyo leader would head a Salvation Army–type mission to Mongolia. Since Japanese Shinto was not a suitable religion for those circumstances, Onisaburo formulated, on the spot, Omoto Buddhism. He designated himself as the Maitreya Incarnation Dalai Lama (as opposed to the Avalokiteshvara Incarnation Dalai Lama in Tibet); Matsumura, the second in command, was nominated as the Panchen Lama. All members took regal Chinese monikers as well. Morihei's was Wang Shou-kao, King of Protectors.

Superstitious, naive, and stubborn, Lu was a very poor choice as a collaborator in such a grand scheme. He was totally dazzled by Onisaburo—the physiognomists and soothsayers he had secretly retained to evaluate the Omoto-kyo patriarch reported that not only did the Japanese lama possess the thirty-three marks of a living buddha, but he had a star-shaped birthmark on his back and stigmata to boot. Thus, Lu was absolutely certain that this messiah would lead them all to the Promised Land. Furthermore, he could not discern that Chang was merely pretending to support his cause; Lu would dig his own grave, Chang correctly calculated, and Chang would be free of a pesky rival.

Onisaburo was in fact reluctant to get involved with Lu since Omoto-kyo espoused nonviolence, but Yano persuaded him that the bandit Lu was really a kind of Manchurian Robin Hood. The ill-fated party started out for Mongolia at the beginning of March. Lu arranged for them the loan of two of the very few automobiles in the entire province. Unfortunately, paved roads were not part of the bargain, and the group would have made faster progress on foot over the endless procession of rocky roads, muddy fields, and icy rivers that awaited them. In one car crash, the windshield shattered and driver Morihei sustained numerous deep cuts across his face. After experiencing innumerable breakdowns, dreadful weather, near starvation, and continual harassment by local authorities, police, army patrols, and wild dogs, the party arrived at the border town of Taonan. Following a brief rest and consultation with the Japanese agents operating there, they proceeded toward the Mongolian holy city of Ulanhot.

As an ancient center of Tantric Buddhism, Ulanhot was the perfect stage for Onisaburo's flamboyant style of religion. He made his entrance on a snow-white horse, and the local populace was captivated by his lordly presence and grand manner of conducting prayer services and meditation rituals. (Onisaburo had a good ear for languages and he was fluent enough in Mongolian to deliver simple yet dramatic sermons.) In addition to his skill as a psychologist and mind reader, Onisaburo's knowledge of medicine and veterinary science put him in good stead healing the painful but, for the most part, minor illnesses that plagued the populace and its livestock.

A rumor, encouraged by Onisaburo, circulated that the lama was in fact a Mongolian, not a Japanese, who had been born in Mongolia and taken to Japan when he was six years old; Onisaburo had now returned to his homeland, as a second Genghis Khan, to guide his fellow Mongols to independence.

For his part, Onisaburo was enthralled with the unlimited vistas of the Mongolian landscape. When he visited the Great Kingan Range he was moved to compose this verse:

> *Heaven? Earth?*
> *Or the vast sea?*
> *I cannot tell—*
> *Pure moonbeams over*
> *The vast plains of Mongolia.*

Onisaburo, however, was dismayed by the corruption of the local Mongolian lamas, including the so-called Living Buddhas. They appeared to be an unseemly gang of greedy, rapacious, and syphilitic imposters. Morihei gave lavish performances of chinkon-kishin techniques and, utilizing his knowledge of Japanese massage techniques, applied the laying on of hands to cure illness. He was ridiculed by Mongolian thugs because of his small size—they laughed out loud when he was introduced as the much bigger Onisaburo's bodyguard—but he demonstrated his prowess as the King of Protectors by causing his tormentors to collapse by merely touching them—they were unaware that he attacked their vital pressure points—and word spread that Morihei was a frightful sorcerer. Morihei gave formal instruction in the martial arts to selected military men (although some complained, "What good is Jujutsu against bullets?"). He must have squared off against Chinese boxers, but he left no record, either oral or written, of these encounters.

Even though Onisaburo and Morihei were received enthusiastically by the general public, skeptical warlords wanted more proof of the Grand Lama's divinity before committing themselves unreservedly to Lu's cause.

"How about conjuring up a rainstorm?" Lu said to Onisaburo. "That shouldn't be too difficult for a Living Buddha."

Onisaburo was reluctant, but Matsumura volunteered to act as his proxy. The two secluded themselves for a week to prepare for the important event. On the scheduled day, the two were taken to a parade ground where a large crowd had gathered to see if the two lamas had what it takes. As an added challenge there was not a single cloud in the deep-blue Mongolian sky. Inexplicably, Matsumura managed to pray up a storm—clouds rose out of nowhere, thunder roared, and the rain came pouring down. When the photographer sighed, "Well, I guess that ruins today's commemorative picture," Onisaburo leapt up, went out into the middle of the field, raised his arms to heaven, and let loose with a tremendous kototama shout. The wind died down, the sky cleared, the sun returned, and the photograph was taken.

However impressive, even this performance did not stem the tide threatening to engulf Lu and his forces. The arms promised by Yano failed to materialize, and Chang denounced Lu's plot to overthrow the government. As the Chinese army and its bandit allies began pressing in on the rebel, Lu decided to set up a different base in the southern town of Paiyintala (also romanized as Baiyantala, present-day Tungliao). Onisaburo, alerted by a "divine messenger," warned Lu of the danger awaiting the warlord there. "If we are attacked," Lu countered, "Your Holiness can call down a flood and drown our enemies."

Faced with no alternative, the Japanese group reluctantly accompanied Lu to Paiyintala. Ambushed by bandits several times along the way, Morihei fought off the attacks by returning gunfire, wielding his sword, or in deadly hand-to-hand combat; the party miraculously survived, intact, finally arriving at the gates of Paiyintala. Much to their chagrin, authorities there had them arrested and bound, and their valuables confiscated (including Onisaburo's platinum watch, his priceless Japanese sword, and a small fortune in gold). They were held captive for a time but then unexpectedly released and taken to the town's best inn.

Lu and his lieutenants, arrested earlier as well, were there too; the entire group was wined and dined and women were brought in for the soldiers. A special bath was prepared, and everyone was treated to a shave and haircut. Despite the lavish treatment, Onisaburo and Lu were grim—they knew that it was an old Chinese custom to fete condemned men the night before execution.

Early in the morning, Lu and his men, 137 in all, were roused one by one and taken out to be shot by the Chinese army. Perhaps alerted to Morihei's reputation as a superlative bodyguard, a large contingent of soldiers, their weapons drawn, burst into the rooms housing the Japanese. The prisoners were cast into leg and arm irons and paraded to the execution grounds, making their way through a pile of bloody corpses.

Onisaburo was calm, almost jovial, considering their dire straits. He sang out:

Off to wed the
Heavenly maidens
Awaiting us in Paradise,
This firing squad serving
As our matchmaker!

Morihei, a warrior trained to fight to the death but now being asked to lay down his life without resistance, was the most agitated of the group. "After we are killed, be sure to keep your souls close to mine so I can direct you to paradise," Onisaburo counseled his companions and then recited another impromptu verse to stir their spirits:

Even though our bodies
Will wither away here
On the plains of Mongolia,
Our deeds as Japanese patriots
Will never fade.

At this dramatic juncture (according to Omoto-kyo versions), a messenger arrived with word of a last-minute reprieve. Actually, it is almost certain that the Chinese had no real intention of executing the Japanese party and that they were merely toying with them. The long delay between the killings of Lu's men and the planned execution of the Japanese group was ascribed implausibly to faulty weapons. Surely, the Chinese army could have found at least one weapon in working order if it truly wanted to dispose of Onisaburo's group. Since the Japanese army was quick to avenge the deaths of any of their countrymen—even the likes of the stigmatized Onisaburo—the risk of Japanese intervention was too great. The Chinese may have been trying to score points with the Japanese as well by returning the fugitive Onisaburo.

Onisaburo and his group were released to the custody of the local Japanese consul and under Japanese military escort they were returned to Japan at the end of July 1924. Onisaburo's bond was revoked for this escapade and he was imprisoned, only to be released on bail again in November. Onisaburo was typically unfazed by the failure of his grand mission to establish heaven on earth—"The timing was just not right." Morihei was more than a little bitter about the manner in which the Omoto-kyo leader had been used by various political factions to advance their own interests.

Not surprisingly, Morihei was forever altered by his many face-to-face encounters with death during the Great Mongolian Adventure. He was particularly affected by this incident:

> As we neared Paiyintala we were trapped in a valley and showered with bullets. Miraculously, I could sense the direction of the projectiles—beams of light indicated their paths of flight—and I was able to dodge the bullets. The ability to sense an attack is what the ancient masters meant by anticipation. If one's mind is steady and pure, one can instantly perceive an attack and counter—that, I realized, is the essence of aiki."

Morihei also had several intense mystical experiences during the prayer fasts and purification rites he performed in Mongolia with Onisaburo, in which he felt the gods speaking to him directly.

Morihei's Enlightenment

Although Morihei's profound experiences in Mongolia made him a more considerate and less gruff person in social situations, he intensified his training in the martial arts, arming his disciples with live blades and instructing them to attack full force. Once again, Morihei spent much time in seclusion in the mountains of Kumano, engaging in long prayer fasts, purification in the Nachi Falls, and internalization of martial art techniques. Morihei later told his disciples, "Prior to my adventures in Mongolia I was obsessed with physical power and technical skill; after I returned to Japan I began searching for the essence of Budo, its true spirit."

Back at Ayabe, strange things began to stir. Every evening, Morihei's wife would hear an eerie *saaa* sound drifting down from the mountains where her husband was training. (Omoto-kyo believers were convinced that Morihei was being taught swordsmanship there by a ferocious tengu gremlin.) In the morning, the high grass near Morihei's house was parted and bent as if some huge beast had passed through. During the day, the household altar would rattle and roll, emitting high-pitched noises.

In the spring of 1925, forty-two-year-old Morihei was transformed by a divine vision. Morihei gave different accounts of the event over the years, and, in his old age, seems to have gradually fused several separate incidents together to form this final version:

> One day a naval officer visiting Ayabe challenged Morihei to a Kendo match. Morihei consented but remained unarmed. The officer, a high-ranking swordsman, was naturally offended at this affront to his ability and lashed out at Morihei furiously, but Morihei easily escaped the officer's repeated strikes and thrusts. When the exhausted officer finally conceded defeat, he asked Morihei his secret. "Just prior to your attacks, a beam of light flashed before my eyes, revealing the intended direction and allowing me to evade them."
>
> Following the contest, Morihei went out into the garden to draw from the well to wash the sweat from his hands and face. Suddenly Morihei started to tremble and

then fell, immobilized. The ground beneath his feet began to vibrate, and he was bathed with rays of pure light streaming down from heaven. A golden mist engulfed his body, causing, he said, all of his petty deceit to vanish. He imagined himself assuming the form of a golden being; the inner workings of the cosmos appeared to him in perfect clarity. Morihei said of this experience: "I saw that I am the universe. All at once I understood the nature of creation; the way of a warrior is to manifest divine love, a spirit that embraces and nurtures all things. I saw the entire universe as my abode, and the sun, moon, and stars as my intimate friends. Tears of gratitude streamed down my face.

Regardless of whether we interpret this enlightenment experience rationally as the culmination of long years of supreme effort coupled with natural ability and superhuman strength or accept it as a truly divine revelation, Morihei was henceforth an invincible warrior manifesting wondrous power.

Morihei's Marvelous Techniques

Following Morihei's enlightenment experience, Omoto-kyo psychics swore that they saw rays emanating from his body; he was also capable of leaping incredible distances, up and over attackers, and displacing enormously heavy boulders. He could dodge any kind of strike or blow, and down any type of opponent.

Such amazing feats began to attract national attention. In addition to the military men who trained at Morihei's dojo in Ayabe, a number of college athletes came from Tokyo to challenge "Japan's Number-One Martial Artist." When rugged Shutaro Nishimura, captain of Waseda University's famed Judo club, heard Onisaburo introduce Morihei as the greatest martial artist alive, Nishimura thought to himself, "Is this some kind of joke? How can this middle-aged country bumpkin be the strongest man in Japan?" The brash Nishimura requested a match with Morihei but as soon as he attempted to grab the middle-aged country bumpkin, Nishimura suddenly found himself flat on his back. Not sure exactly what hit him, Nishimura leapt up. Morihei folded a piece of paper and waved it in front of Nishimura's startled face. "Grab if you can," Morihei challenged. No matter how quickly Nishimura moved, he could not catch the piece of paper; on the contrary, he was continually spun to the mat. A final all-out attack aimed directly at Morihei also failed—Nishimura looked up from the floor at the smiling Morihei and wondered, "Can there really be a martial art in which one downs his attacker with a laugh?"

During intensive training sessions conducted in the woods, Nishimura and a few other students would share a little hut with Morihei. At night, they could never tell if Morihei was asleep or awake. As soon as anyone moved toward him, he would bolt upright, eyes wide open. In the morning, however, he seemed perfectly refreshed. They were miles away from anyone else and without a telephone, but Morihei would astound them by announcing suddenly, "I just learned that Mr. So-and-so will be arriving in thirty minutes." Sure enough, Mr. So-and-so was there thirty minutes later. Nishimura once attacked Morihei full-force with a thick wooden sword; Morihei's parry of the blow, barely perceptible, broke Nishimura's sword in two.

Tales such as these, and the ease with which Morihei's women students handled mashers and drunks, helped spread the word and in the fall of 1925 the distinguished admiral Isamu Takeshita, who had become an enthusiastic supporter of Morihei, arranged for him to give a special demonstration in Tokyo before a select group of influential people. Morihei performed mostly spear techniques, and when asked what school he was affiliated with, he replied that his style was "natural and independent."

One of the spectators stated, "In the old days, it was said that the master Genba Tawarabashi could lift and toss twenty sacks of rice with his spear in rapid succession. Can you do likewise?"

"Let's see," replied Morihei.

Twenty 125-pound sacks loaded with rice were carried into the garden (the demonstration was being held at a huge private mansion). The sacks were divided into two piles facing respectively east and west. Morihei alternately speared the top sack in each pile, lifted it up, and then tossed it in the opposite corner, ending up with two neat piles facing east and west, without spilling a grain.

After this impressive performance, Count Yamamoto, a former prime minister, requested that Morihei conduct a twenty-one-day training session at Aoyama Palace for members of the imperial family and their bodyguards. The training session proceeded smoothly the first week, but then several government officials, uneasy with Morihei's Omoto-kyo connections, protested. Although Yamamoto and several other senior statesmen vouched for Morihei, he himself was so peeved by the insinuations that he canceled the remaining lessons and announced in an indignant huff, "I'm returning to Ayabe to resume farming."

Morihei went back to Ayabe, but in the spring of 1926 Admiral Takeshita again persuaded him to come to Tokyo, assuring him that there would be no further misunderstandings. Morihei, not fully convinced, reluctantly agreed. After his arrival in the capital, he stayed briefly at the home of a business tycoon in the Yotsuya section of town and then at a small dojo on the property of another magnate in Shinagawa.

Morihei, however, was not well. One day he collapsed after training and appeared to be near death. While unconscious, Morihei had another vision, this time of a lovely rainbow-clad maiden riding on a heavenly tortoise; he interpreted this as an omen of divine favor.

His doctors thought otherwise and pronounced his condition terminal. Even though Morihei did not have stomach cancer as feared, bleeding ulcers and extreme exhaustion made his health precarious. For someone possessed of super-human strength, Morihei was in surprisingly delicate health during the latter half of his life. He suffered constantly from severe stomach and liver disorders. Morihei himself placed the blame for his weak stomach on damage caused during a salt-water drinking contest he had with a yoga practitioner when he lived in Ayabe; it also appears that he contracted some chronic illness during the Great Mongolian Adventure.

Onisaburo met with Morihei in Tokyo and, alarmed at his trusted disciple's ghastly complexion, solicitously ordered him back to Ayabe to recuperate. Immediately after speaking with Onisaburo—who was under constant police surveil-lance—Morihei was accosted by two plainclothesmen and taken to police headquarters where he was questioned about one of his students, "a dangerous right-wing radical."

"He comes to the dojo to train and that's all I know about him," Morihei protested. "I've done nothing wrong. Why are you treating me like this?" Morihei was released and, dis-gusted at such rude treatment, returned to his family in Ayabe.

Six months later, Takeshita and Morihei's other supporters were at Ayabe once more, pleading with Morihei to settle permanently in Tokyo. Onisaburo, too, encouraged Morihei to leave Ayabe to carry his message to the world at large. A nice home was secured for Morihei and his family in the Shiba Shirogane section of Tokyo. The family arrived in Tokyo in October of 1927, but Morihei misplaced his wallet somewhere between Ayabe and Tokyo, so the family arrived at their new home penniless. Morihei, too proud to tell any-one about the predicament, said nothing. Luckily, an obser-vant acquaintance noticed the shortfall and discovered the reason for the lack of cash. Adequate provisions were imme-diately provided but thereafter Mrs. Ueshiba handled the money.

Morihei's indifference to financial matters created endless troubles for his family. He exhausted his huge patrimony on the pursuit of his martial art and religious studies; he gave away several priceless swords to acquaintances who merely expressed their admiration for them; and he would refuse large, no-strings-attached donations if he happened to have enough money on hand at the time. Some of the wealthiest men in Japan were among his patrons, yet he never treated them any differently from the most impoverished live-in disciples. All the money he did receive was placed on the Shinto altar. When operating funds were low, Mrs. Ueshiba was permitted to "borrow" the money from the gods. Except for a few really flush years before the war, when Morihei's yearly income from teaching (including a cabinet member–level salary from the government) was around $200,000 in today's money, the gods were frequently broke, and Mrs. Ueshiba was forced to pass the word that immediate assistance was necessary to keep the Tokyo dojo going. (Later on, the disciples in Iwama, scolded by Morihei that he "was not teaching them for money," started a fund of their own for the upkeep of the buildings and other expenses.)

In Tokyo, Morihei developed an interest in the teachings of Bonji Kawatsura (1862–1929), founder of the Misogi School of ancient Shinto. A number of Kawatsura's ritual purification techniques were adopted by Morihei for use as preparatory exercises in his Budo training. A temporary dojo was constructed in a remodeled billiard room in the Shimazu mansion. Within a year the family was obliged to move to larger quarters in Shiba Mita and then again to a bigger place in Shiba Kuruma, next to the famous burial site of the Forty-Seven Ronin. When it became evident that the makeshift dojo could no longer handle the crush of trainees—people had to line up and wait for a turn on the mat—some of Morihei's wealthy supporters drew up plans for the construction of a large training hall. Land was donated in the Wakamatsu neighborhood of Tokyo and a building fund established. The impatient Morihei often visited the dojo site to help speed up the construction. The workers were astounded by the heavy loads of lumber Morihei could haul and the huge boulders he could displace.

While the dojo was under construction, Morihei and his family leased a house in Meijiro. There he had two memorable encounters.

Memorable Encounters

The first encounter was with General Miura, a hero of the Russo-Japanese War. Miura was famed for cutting down over fifty Russian soldiers with his officer's sword, despite having been run through the chest by a Russian bayonet. Miura had once been a student of Sokaku as well, and he wanted to see for himself if Morihei was the genuine article.

After an exchange of pleasantries, Miura asked for a demonstration. Absolutely fearless and secretly harboring a desire to humiliate Morihei, the general attacked with all his might. In spite of his steely determination and martial prowess, Miura was completely stymied by Morihei. Miura apologized deeply for his rash behavior and begged to be admitted as a student: "Your techniques are a world apart from those of the Daito Ryu. It is true Budo. Please enroll me as your disciple."

Even though Morihei could handle Miura with no difficulty, the general still wondered how well Morihei would fare against a no-holds-barred multiple attack. Miura eventually arranged for a demonstration by Morihei to be given at the Toyama Military Academy. After the demonstration, Miura informed Morihei that the cadets wanted a full display of his power.

Urged on by Miura, the cocky cadets challenged Morihei with wooden bayonets. They counseled him to wear protective armor, but Morihei refused: "It won't be necessary. Are you going to attack one at a time?"

"Of course!"

"That's too easy. In my Budo, we expect attackers from all directions. Come at me together!"

Hesitant as they were at first, only one cadet stepped forward. After he went flying the cadets lost all reserve and rushed in, only to find themselves upended in a flash.

The second encounter was with Jigoro Kano, the founder of Kodokan Judo, who paid a visit to the Meijiro dojo in October 1930. Kano, a cosmopolitan, English-speaking intellectual, was in most respects the diametrical opposite of the old-fashioned mystic Morihei, but he too was dazzled by Morihei's techniques. "This is the ideal Budo—true Judo," Kano exclaimed after witnessing Morihei's performance. (A disciple of Kano who heard this remark later asked his teacher, "Does that mean what we are doing is fake Judo?") Kano humbly asked Morihei to accept two of his senior students as trainees. Morihei agreed and Kano had them regularly report to him the results of their study with the master.

The Kobukan

The new dojo, named Kobukan, opened in March of 1931. Finally settled in one place teaching Aiki Budo, Morihei became the center of a whirl of activity. Trainees clamored to be accepted as students, and Morihei was highly selective, requiring a proper introduction, two responsible sponsors, and, most important, a personal interview. During the interview, Morihei invited the prospective candidate to attack "in any manner you wish." No matter what attack the candidate employed, he would end up on the ground, unsure of how he got there. One trainee, named Yukawa, said of the experience, "I grabbed Morihei but immediately my body went numb and I crashed to the mat." If Morihei did not like what he saw, the candidate was immediately rejected without explanation. If, on the other hand, Morihei perceived that the petitioner was sincere, he accepted him or her unconditionally. There was no set system of fees, but every live-in disciple offered some type of payment, whether in the form of cash, food, supplies, or work. Practice sessions ran from six to seven o'clock and nine to ten o'clock in the morning, then two to four o'clock in the afternoon and seven to eight o'clock in the evening.

The live-in disciples slept in the dojo, took care of the cleaning and other chores, and served as Morihei's attendants. Live-in disciples had to be literally on guard at all times. If Morihei caught them out of position—for example, talking on the telephone too intently, or entering a room or turning a corner without proper caution—they received a sharp reprimand. He would demand answers to such questions as, "How many steps is it from here to the front door of the dojo? You walk that distance every day and a martial artist should always be totally familiar with his surroundings." He would advise them, "Avoid sleeping on the upper floors of a building so you will not get caught going down a flight of stairs in the dark. And before sleeping make sure that there are no heavy objects that may fall on you during an earthquake."

Although the following incident occurred after the war, it illustrates Morihei's dictum that training covers all aspects of life. The chief instructor of the Hombu (headquarters) Dojo returned from an overseas tour with a stylish leather jacket, at the time a valuable object, unattainable in Japan. It was stolen from the changing room, and the furious instructor summoned all the live-in trainees to berate them for their unpardonable inattentiveness. Morihei strolled by and wanted to know the reason for the commotion. When he was told what happened, Morihei said, "Stolen, was it?" He walked silently around the group of seated disciples and then, much to everyone's surprise, barked at the chief instructor, "It is *you* who are at fault." So saying, Morihei turned his back on them and walked out of the hall, leaving everyone to ponder the meaning of his words.

Later on, a puzzled disciple asked Morihei to explain. "Don't you see?" Morihei asked. "A martial artist should never be a show-off or attached to material possessions. That kind of attitude creates 'openings' that others can exploit. The chief instructor let his possessiveness get the better of him, and lost his presence of mind."

In the evenings, the live-in disciples took turns massaging Morihei's shoulders, back, and legs. Morihei encouraged his students to study *shiatsu* and other traditional healing arts; "old time martial artists really knew a lot about the body," he told them. While he was being massaged, Morihei liked to listen to tales of the brave samurai of old, and sometimes he would act out the fight scenes for the benefit of his young charges.

Since Morihei was continually experimenting with new forms and developing novel techniques, there was no systematic step-by-step instruction. The trainees worked on whatever Morihei happened to be researching at the moment. One disciple recalls that Morihei dreamed up new techniques in his sleep because he would sometimes rouse them at two o'clock in the morning to try out his latest innovations.

In addition to teaching at the Kobukan, Takeda, and various branch dojos, Morihei instructed at the Toyama (Spy) Academy, the Naval Academy, the Military Staff College, and the Military Police Academy.

In the summer of 1932 the Dainihon Budo Senyo Kai (Society for the Promotion of Japanese Martial Arts) was established under the auspices of the Omoto-kyo organization, with Morihei acting as chief instructor. The main dojo of this society was located in Takeda, a mountain village in Hyogo Prefecture. An abandoned sake brewery was turned into a boot camp to train the rapidly expanding Omoto-kyo People's Militia. Morihei instructed there during the summers.

Morihei recruited members for the Budo Senyo Kai at Omoto-kyo gatherings by proclaiming: "You young fellows these days have no starch. If any of you think you can take me on, come up here." Invariably, four or five youngsters would leap to the challenge and join the organization after being thrown across the room by Morihei.

The training at remote Takeda was particularly severe, each day full of roughhouse martial art practice and heavy farm work. The following shows the daily schedule there.

5:00 AM	rise and farm work
6:30 AM	morning prayers and meditation
7:00 AM	breakfast
8:00–9:00 AM	Omoto-kyo lecture
9:00–11:00 AM	Budo training
11:00 AM–2:00 PM	lunch and rest
2:00–3:00 PM	Budo training
3:00–4:30 PM	Omoto-kyo lecture
5:00 PM	bath
6:30 PM	dinner
7:00–9:30 PM	informal Budo training
10:00 PM	lights out

It was an all-or-nothing, do-or-die atmosphere at Takeda, and soon there was a breach between the fervent Omoto-kyo believers preparing for a holy mission and the non-Omoto-kyo participants who did not share the faith. Morihei was more or less able to defuse the explosive situation, but things thereafter remained tense.

Morihei was also engaged in the study of sword techniques during this period, going so far as to set up a separate Kendo division at the Kobukan. Morihei's adopted son (and son-in-law), Kiyoshi Nakakura, number-one disciple of the famous Kendo master Hakudo Nakayama, led the Kendo training. (Nakakura's lack of enthusiasm for his father-in-law's Omoto-kyo beliefs coupled with unresolved marital problems caused him to leave the Ueshiba family within a few years of his adoption.)

In order to really test Morihei, Nakakura and Junichi

Haga, another talented swordsman, devised a plan to ambush him in the dojo before training began. They would attack Morihei in unison from the front and from the back. Everything went exactly as planned, but Morihei instantly countered their coordinated attacks—Nakakura went flying across the room and Haga was pinned helplessly on the mat. They never questioned Morihei's ability again.

One disciple noticed that Morihei always evaded to the right when he attacked his teacher with a sword. He tried to cross Morihei up by directly lashing out in that direction. This time Morihei did not move an inch. "What on earth are you doing?" he teased the disciple.

Professional boxers and wrestlers, too, came to test Morihei. "Piston" Horiguchi, former bantamweight world champion owning the "fastest hands in boxing," tried to land a punch on Morihei's jaw. Morihei caught the punch in a viselike grip; the pain of the grip forced Horiguchi to his knees. Giant pro wrestlers from abroad stormed the dojo, attempted to floor Morihei with flying drop kicks or to immobilize him with their favorite holds. Morihei tossed the behemoths around as if they were rag dolls. One foreign wrestler told him, "You are amazing! Come to America with me and we will make a million dollars."

The Second Omoto-kyo Incident

On the morning of December 8, 1935, five hundred heavily armed police officers stormed the main Omoto-kyo centers and arrested Onisaburo and his chief aides on charges of lese majesty and fomenting armed rebellion. Morihei, too, was a prime target of the crackdown—the existence of the Budo Senyo Kai, which the government considered a dangerous paramilitary organization, was specifically cited as one of the factors justifying the raid—and a warrant for his arrest was issued by the Kyoto Police Department. Morihei was in Osaka at the time, perhaps having been alerted in advance of the raid by his disciples in the police agency. The police chief in Osaka, Kenji Tomita (later to become secretary-general of the Konoe cabinet), was one of those disciples and he arranged for his teacher to be politely interrogated—albeit for twelve hours—and then released. When the Kyoto Police Department insisted on Morihei's detainment, Tomita had Morihei bundled off to Sonezaki, where the police chief there, another student of Morihei, sheltered Morihei in his own home.

It seems that Morihei was under house arrest for a time but his many influential supporters in the police agency and the government were able to keep him out of jail, primarily by convincing the prosecutors that he was too valuable an asset as a martial art instructor to imprison. Many members of Omoto-kyo were bitter about the special treatment afforded Morihei but it was Onisaburo himself who had warned Morihei of the impending crackdown. Onisaburo told him to resign as chairman of the Budo Senyo Kai in the summer of 1935 and distance himself from all Omoto-kyo institutions. Also, Onisaburo evidently told the prosecutors that Morihei was never a member of the religion's inner circle. To Morihei's credit, he refused to denounce Onisaburo even when his supporters in the government urged him to do so: "Onisaburo is my teacher, and I will never renounce him to save my own skin."

The suppression of Omoto-kyo was one of the harshest and most thorough of a dissident movement in Japanese history, in spite of the fact that no one in the organization resisted and not a single weapon or bomb was found. Everything of value at the Ayabe and Kameoka compounds was seized and auctioned off; fifteen thousand laborers were set to work dynamiting and torching every Omoto-kyo building; the remaining debris was set ablaze (the fire smoldered for a week), and then the ashes were bulldozed into the earth. Anything remotely associated with Omoto-kyo was either burned, crushed, or tossed into the sea. Omoto-kyo leaders were tortured, and thousands of Omoto-kyo members lost their jobs.

(Onisaburo was imprisoned for more than six and a half years before finally being convicted of lese majesty—he was found innocent of inciting rebellion—in 1942. During his long years of imprisonment, Onisaburo's antic sense of humor never deserted him. Onisaburo openly masturbated every day in prison. When the guards demanded to know what he was doing, Onisaburo replied, "I'm just making do with what is on hand!" When prison authorities informed his wife, Sumi, about his "shameful" behavior, she just smiled and said, "Sounds just like him." Onisaburo seems to have been subject to involuntary erections right up to the end of his life; on occasion, he would playfully stick his rigid member through holes in paper doors to startle his female followers. The ladies would sometimes retaliate, though, giving the offending member a good tweak. Then seventy-two years old and in poor health, he was released on bond. In 1945 the new government administration exonerated Onisaburo of all charges and he was a free man. His supporters encouraged him to sue the government and seek compensation for wrongful imprisonment, but Onisaburo refused, saying "Everyone suffered during this terrible war, and any compensation I receive will just increase the taxes of the already heavily burdened population." Onisaburo once again started from scratch to build a new utopian community. However, the Great Guru finally succumbed to death, the one obstacle no human being can overcome, in 1948.)

Amazing Feats

There are dozens of amazing tales told about Morihei during the prewar period. Morihei encouraged his disciples to try to catch him off guard, promising a teaching license to anyone who could do so. Every time a disciple thought there was a chance to get Morihei—when he was dozing on a train, had his back turned at a banquet, when he was praying intently at a shrine, or even when he was in the toilet—the master would fix his eyes on the disciple and counter with this preemptive strike: "The gods just whispered to me that you intend to whack me on the head. You wouldn't be thinking of doing something like that would you?"

Other times, the live-in disciples would sneak out at night, observing the utmost caution to cover their tracks. Despite the painstaking stealth, Morihei would invariably ask the next morning, "Did you fellows have a good time last night?" More embarrassingly, Morihei would say to a disciple who had stayed in but played in his mind, "You had quite an erotic dream last night." Once during a training session Morihei said to several of his students, "The Korean couple down the road are having a big fight. Go and break it up before someone gets hurt." One time when he was staying in Osaka, Morihei received word that Mrs. Ueshiba was seriously ill. He planned to return to Tokyo on the first train in the morning, but in the middle of the night he woke up and said to his attendant, "Cancel the trip. The danger is over." A telegram arrived in the morning bearing news of Mrs. Ueshiba's improvement.

Once a sculptor was commissioned to do a bust of Morihei's muscular upper torso. When the model was finished, Morihei checked the back side of the bust and said to the sculptor, "This muscle and this muscle are not quite right." Upon closer examination, the sculptor was shocked to find it so. Morihei knew the exact configuration of his back even though he could not, of course, see it.

As soon as Morihei entered a dojo, he paid his respects to the Shinto altar. After doing so at one dojo, he called the instructor over and berated him: "Why did you neglect to chant the morning prayers today? The god here is lonely!"

Although an invaluable resource for a martial artist, Morihei's ultrasensitivity complicated daily living. He could not board certain electrical trains because the strong current gave him unbearable headaches. Nor could he tolerate bathing in water used by others—standard practice in Japan—because he could sense the character of each person who had bathed before him. If a disciple so much as dipped a single finger in the water to test the temperature Morihei would know. Thus, each bath had to be freshly prepared. He was also irritated by the insects landing on paper doors or restless trainees sleeping several doors distant.

Some of the tales are simply incredible. In his memoirs, Gozo Shioda has provided detailed, eyewitness accounts of several such miraculous events. Once when Shioda was traveling with Morihei they were walking up the steps to a train platform when a man at the top of the stairs tripped and tumbled back straight toward them. Morihei shouted and the man "unfell," somehow landing back on his feet at the top of the stairs.

Military people often came to the Kobukan to observe demonstrations. One day a group of marksmen showed up and Morihei said to them provokingly, "Bullets cannot touch me." The offended marksmen demanded that Morihei prove himself. Morihei agreed to sign a release form, absolving the marksmen of all liability, and a showdown was set at their home firing range. Shioda had often been awed by Morihei's magic, but this time he said to himself, "Master Ueshiba has gone too far. We'd better start preparing for his funeral." Mrs. Ueshiba pleaded with her husband to give up this foolhardy stunt, but Morihei told her not to worry.

On the appointed day, Morihei showed up at the range with Shioda. He placed himself as the target in the middle of the firing range, about seventy-five feet in front of the squad. The marksmen took aim and fired. There was a tremendous noise, much like a thunderclap, and several marksmen were swept from their feet. Morihei, completely unharmed, was suddenly standing *behind* them. Totally nonplussed, everyone asked Morihei to please repeat the miracle. Once more, Morihei set himself up as the target. Aware that something supernatural was about to occur, Shioda glued his eyes to Morihei's figure. The guns went off, lights flashed, there was a huge roar, the marksmen went flying, and again Morihei ended up safely behind the firing squad. Shioda had been unable to discern a single thing.

"How on earth did you do that?" Shioda asked Morihei on the way home. "My purpose on earth is not fully accomplished yet so nothing can harm me," Morihei replied cryptically. "Once my task is completed, then it will be time to go, but until then I'm perfectly safe from harm." (Later, when Japan was being bombarded by B-29s during the war, Morihei told his disciples, "When the bombing starts stick close to me and you won't be hurt.")

Shioda was acquainted with a sharpshooter named Teijiro Sato, an eccentric fellow (not unlike Morihei) who hid out in the mountains living as a hunter. Whenever Sato appeared at a firing range, he scored one hundred bull's-eyes out of one hundred shots, and people swore that they had never seen him miss a shot at game in the wild either. Told of Morihei's face-off with the military firing squad, Sato said to Shioda, "He may be able to dodge the bullets of those cockeyed novices but he will never be able to stay out of my sights!" Shioda dutifully arranged for the two wizards to square off against each other. Morihei plunked himself down in the middle of the dojo; Sato raised his rifle, finger on the trigger. "Stop!" Morihei yelled out. "You've got me. Without firing your bullet you scored a direct hit." Morihei later said to Shioda, "Sato is a real master. There is no way you can escape a marksman who 'shoots without shooting.'"

Morihei's live-in disciples had been after him to show them some real *ninja* stealth and Morihei finally relented. Morihei had them surround him armed with wooden swords and sticks. "Attack!" he commanded. They felt a stream of air and then heard Morihei call out to them from the far end of the hall, at least twenty-five feet away. When they requested another performance, Morihei yelled, "Are you trying to kill me just to entertain yourselves? Such feats can shorten life by five or ten years!"

In 1941 the Imperial Household Agency requested a command performance of Morihei's Aiki Budo on the grounds of the palace. (Hirohito did not practice Aiki Budo but several other members of the imperial family did.) The week before the scheduled demonstration Morihei was stricken with a severe gastrointestinal ailment (such attacks were not infrequent in Morihei's mature years); he vomited continuously and was extremely dehydrated by the day of the demonstration. Despite his grave condition, Morihei refused to cancel the appearance. As they carried him to the hall and helped him into his training outfit, the two disciples accompanying Morihei, Yukawa and Shioda, looked at the deathly pale, emaciated face of their teacher and wondered, "How can he possibly give a demonstration in this state? He will never survive."

However, as soon as Morihei entered the imperial hall, he suddenly straightened up and strode briskly toward the center of the room. Yukawa, afraid that his teacher was only functioning at one-tenth his normal strength, held back when he initiated his attack. With his guard down, Yukawa fractured his arm when Morihei threw him with the customary force. Shioda therefore had to take all the break falls for the entire forty-minute demonstration. Shioda recalled, "All I remember seeing was Morihei's blazing eyes, not his body, and I seemed to be enveloped in a purple haze." Once out of the hall, all three collapsed and spent the rest of the week recovering in bed.

Morihei served as the chief Budo instructor at Kenkoku University in Manchukuo, an institution established by the Japanese to train Japanese and Chinese officials to serve in the puppet empire founded by the Japanese in 1932 and headed by Pu-i, the "Last Emperor." Aiki Budo was a required course for all of the students enrolled there, and Morihei visited Manchukuo regularly to teach at the university. During one demonstration Morihei had a match with Tenryu, a former professional Sumo champion. The huge Tenryu was totally unable to budge little Morihei, and then Morihei pinned him to the floor with one finger. Tenryu went on to become one of Morihei's most devoted students.

Morihei's power was truly mind-boggling but he himself remained modest about his incredible accomplishments. After the war, his young students once asked him, "Master, have you always been undefeated?" Morihei replied:

No, I've experienced failure many times due to inattention and improper attitude. One time I was traveling with my former teacher Sokaku Takeda, running along carrying his baggage, and I nearly collided with an old woman who suddenly crossed my path. I just managed to avoid running into her but from the standpoint of Budo that was a defeat, since I was not paying sufficient attention to my surroundings. Another time, I was conducting a class and while I was showing a basic movement to one of my students, he suddenly reached out and attempted to throw me. I was able to counter the throw at the last moment but I had been temporarily caught off guard. I therefore learned to remain alert even with my own disciples. Once I was challenged by a Sumo wrestler who was only wearing a *mawashi* (loin cloth). His body was so sweaty that I couldn't hold him long enough to pin him. I finally got him down and under control; this experience taught me the technique the old-time martial-art masters called 'catching a slippery eel.' While I was conducting a seminar at a police academy one day, I injured one of the participants who was resisting fiercely. This may have taught him a lesson, according to the old way of thinking, but I resolved thereafter to refine my technique to allow any partner of mine to escape injury since no one should get hurt while practicing Aikido. All of these failures helped me to improve and develop my art.

The Tragedy of World War II

Morihei was actually extremely distressed by the outbreak of war in 1937 with China and then with the United States in 1941. When Morihei had been a soldier in the Russo-Japanese War, the Japanese military behaved as well as fighting men can, and the Japanese army was singled out by the International Red Cross for its fair treatment of civilians and prisoners of war. Over the ensuing years, however, blind nationalism and racist contempt for outsiders turned many military men into heartless brutes who were merciless at cutting down the weak. Morihei was acutely aware of the contradiction between his contention that Budo was a way of love that fostered and preserved life and the massive death and destruction of war. Morihei told his students, "Even in war, the taking of human life is to be avoided as much as possible. It is always a sin to kill. Give your opponents every chance to make peace." His message largely fell on deaf ears and he once complained to his son Kisshomaru, "The military is dominated by reckless fools, ignorant of statesmanship and religious ideas, who slaughter innocent citizens indiscriminately and destroy everything in their path. They act in total contradiction to the will of the gods and they will surely come to a sorry end. True Budo is to nourish life and foster peace, love, and respect, not to blast the world to pieces with weapons." Later on, Morihei often mentioned to his disciples how deeply he suffered when he was obliged to teach military men how to use Budo for destructive purposes during the war. After the war Morihei stated in an interview, "In the old days, Budo was used for destructive purposes—to attack others in order to seize more land and possesions. Japan lost the war because it followed an evil, destructive path. From now on, Budo must be used for constructive purposes."

It has recently come to light that Morihei had valiantly

worked behind the scenes in attempts to prevent war with the United States and to make peace in China—alas, to no avail. Made physically and emotionally ill by the carnage, Morihei, pleading poor health, resigned all his positions, entrusted the operation of the Tokyo dojo to Kisshomaru, and moved to a small farm in Iwama, about one hundred miles north of Tokyo, in the autumn of 1942. In his later years, Morihei intimated that his abrupt move to Iwama was at divine command. An inner voice said to him, "Go to the country, build a shrine dedicated to the Great Spirit of Aiki, and prepare yourself to be the guiding light of a new Japan."

The Move to Iwama

Morihei never cared much for city life, and he had begun acquiring land in Iwama from around 1935 in hope of someday establishing a farm-dojo in the country. By 1942, Morihei's property extended to nearly seventeen acres, a sizable plot in cramped Japan. There were no proper buildings on the property, however, so Morihei purchased a local farmer's shed and had it remodeled into a simple cottage. Visitors from Tokyo were shocked to find Morihei and his wife, who had been literally and figuratively right in the middle of things a short time before, living in such spartan accommodations. Morihei and his wife, on the contrary, were overjoyed to be back in the bosom of Mother Nature.

Morihei always loved farming. In the Iwama fields, Morihei raised rice, potatoes, buckwheat, barley, azuki and soy beans, peanuts, and vegetables, and the yield on his land was considerably higher than that of neighboring farms, even though the soil was not rich. He appreciated the honest labor involved in farming and often told his young students, "Budo training is easy compared to farm work!"

At first, the villagers in Iwama were rather leery of the

"strange fellow in the woods." When Morihei recited his Shinto prayers in the morning, his high-pitched, unearthly voice would carry a mile or more. When he shouted during outdoor training, the force of his cries would sometimes knock birds from the air. Once, during a ceremony at a Buddhist temple, Morihei joined the congregation in the chanting of the Heart Sutra. Although Morihei was chanting in his normal voice, the priest felt as if the sounds rising from Morihei were pounding him solidly on the back.

During the rest of the war years, Morihei slowly recuperated—he was ill as long as his country was ill—and he concentrated on constructing the Aiki Shrine and outdoor dojo at Iwama. In 1942, Morihei formally designated his teaching as Aikido, the Way of Harmony. The war reached its tragic conclusion on August 15, 1945, with millions of soldiers and civilians dead, thousands sick and maimed, all the major cities (with the exception of Kyoto) in ruins. Morihei later told his disciples: "When the war ended, I fell deathly ill, into a trance. A celestial maiden appeared to me, surrounded by flames. I moved toward the light but then a Buddhist monk appeared and said to me, 'It is not time for you to go yet. You have a mission to accomplish on earth.'" Morihei recovered his health and was one of the few Japanese who were optimistic about the future. "Don't worry," he consoled his disheartened disciples. "Instead of foolishly waging war, hereafter we will wage peace, the true purpose of Aikido. We will train to prevent war, to abolish nuclear weapons, to protect the environment, and to serve society."

The Spread of Aikido

The introduction of Aikido to the world at large got off to a slow start. Although the Tokyo dojo survived the air raids intact—owing to the heroic efforts of Morihei's son Kisshomaru, who doused the flames constantly threatening to engulf the building—thirty neighborhood families (nearly one hundred people in all) who had been bombed out of their homes were squatting on the premises. Even if the dojo had been usable, the United States Occupation authorities had, in effect, banned the practice of most martial arts, making it difficult to practice openly. Morihei and a few of his disciples were able, though, to train quietly in Iwama despite the prohibition. The dojo there lacked mats, however, and the lights frequently went out due to power outages. One student recalled, "When the lights went out and the dojo was pitch dark, Morihei's glowing eyes were the only thing visible."

In 1948 permission was granted by the Occupation authorities and the Japanese Ministry of Education to organize an Aiki Foundation to promote Aikido, "a martial way dedicated to the fostering of international peace and justice," and in 1949 the Tokyo dojo officially reopened. (It took until 1955 to get the last of the squatters to depart.)

There were few trainees at first. The public transportation system, destroyed by the war, took time to rebuild, and because of the severe food shortage, people did not want to expend energy moving around. Everyone had to toil from morning to night in order to survive, and Morihei's son, Kisshomaru, took an outside job with a securities firm (much to the chagrin of his father—"Why are you working for a bunch of greedy capitalists and amoral speculators?"). As the economic situation improved, Morihei's prewar disciples resumed their training, more new trainees joined the dojo, Kisshomaru was able to return to full-time work for his father, and branches were gradually established all over Japan and at many universities. The first public demonstration of Aikido was held in 1956. Around the same time, foreigners began practicing Aikido seriously, and the art was spread overseas.

A few foreigners, mostly Italian and German nationals plus a couple of professional wrestlers, had practiced Aiki Budo before the war, and some had trained at Kenkoku University in Manchukuo, but the real influx of foreign students began in the early 1960s. There was a certain amount of tension between the Japanese and foreign trainees, which is not surprising considering the outcome of the war and cultural differences. Morihei, however, was very open to foreign trainees and accepted a few as his personal students (over the objections of his Japanese live-in disciples). One foreign student recalled, "When Morihei was around, he lit the place up, and the dojo seemed to sparkle; if he was gone for a while, though, traveling or in Iwama, things seemed to dim."

Compared with the drama and excitement of the previous years, Morihei's postwar career was relatively uneventful. He turned over administration of the Aiki Foundation and the Hombu Dojo to Kisshomaru and senior disciples and devoted himself full-time to the refinement and perfection of the art of Aikido.

In contrast to the restless, frenetic activity of his youth and middle years, Morihei's last years were characterized by a sense of peace and deep spirituality. After the war, Morihei filled his days with Aikido training, prayer and meditation, study of religious texts, farm work, and calligraphy. He once said:

> By secluding myself in Iwama and reducing my involvement in worldly affairs, I have been able to attain a deeper sense of our oneness with nature. I rise each morning at four, purify myself, and then step outdoors to greet the rising sun. I link myself to the cosmos through Aiki and commune with all things—I feel as if I am transformed into the universe itself, breathing in all phenomena. Standing before the altar of heaven and earth, I am in perfect harmony with the Divine. Then I bow in the four directions and pray and meditate before the Aiki Shrine for an hour and a half.

In his final years, Morihei did little direct instructing, teaching instead by example and inspiration. When he did

lead the training, the emphasis was on the spiritual significance of Aikido. When students would ask, "What is this
technique called?" Morihei replied, "Think up a name yourself, the more poetic the better." If they requested, "Please
show us that footwork again," he would tell them, "The secret of Aikido is not in how you move your feet, it is how you
move your mind. I'm not teaching you martial techniques,
I'm teaching you nonviolence." Morihei's lectures occupied
at least half, if not more, of the practice session. Once a
young student, impatient with Morihei's endless philosophiz-
ing, had the temerity to suggest, "Sensei, isn't it time to actually practice a few techniques?" Morihei exploded at such
impudence and stormed out of the dojo. It took much apol-
ogy and a great deal of pleading to get Morihei to teach
again. Morihei constantly reminded his students, "I'm your
guide. Listen to what I say carefully and then experience
Aikido for yourselves."

Morihei divided his time between Iwama and the Tokyo
Hombu Dojo with frequent instruction tours to various parts
of Japan. Morihei sorely tested the mettle of the disciples who
accompanied him on these journeys. He insisted on being at
the train station at least an hour before his scheduled depar-
ture. (His disciples sometimes tried to fool him by setting the
dojo clock ahead an hour.) The heavily laden bag-carrier had
to buy the tickets, get them punched, and try never to take his
eyes off the speedy Morihei, who did his best to lose his attendant—a sort of catch-me-if-you-can martial art game.
(Morihei never bumped into people, no matter how thick the
crowd, making it especially difficult for less agile trainees to
catch up with him.) Once in a while, Morihei would give
both his accompanying disciple and the welcoming party the
slip and hop into a taxi, demanding that the bewildered
driver take him to the "Aikido demonstration" without giving him the place or address, which Morihei did not know.
Worse, Morihei would board a train, suddenly declare that
something was amiss, and jump off just as the train was

pulling away from the platform, thus in effect canceling the scheduled event for that day.

On shorter streetcar rides Morihei would catch falling packages when the car made a sudden stop, berating his disciples for not doing likewise because of inattention. One day the streetcar Morihei was riding on collided with another vehicle. At the instant of impact, Morihei shouted, and the car flipped over and landed upright without injury to any of the passengers.

In spite of the great strain of being Morihei's attendant—one day of being Morihei's attendant was more tiring than a month of hard training—disciples clamored for the honor of accompanying their master. All agree that the experience—carrying his heavy bags, massaging his legs during the trip, preparing a bath of just the right temperature, sleeping outside the door of his room in order to lead the way to the toilet when he rose at night, and seeing him safely back home—was the supreme test of one's ability to keep pace with the master. A disciple could count on losing ten to fifteen pounds during a journey, and one disciple joked that his weight fell as soon as he heard Morihei would be coming. Another disciple said, "The night before the master came to visit he would always appear to me in a dream and immediately start throwing me around the dojo." In 1961, Morihei made his first and only journey to United States territory, a forty-day tour of Hawaii. Here is an interesting tale from Morihei's Hawaiian trip: A local Japanese-American Aikido student sat on the side watching Morihei execute evasive movements against a sword attack. "The attacker is only striking with direct blows so it is easy for the master to escape," the student thought to himself. "If I was up there, I'd thrust and nail him for sure." The practice session ended, and before Morihei left the dojo he walked over to the student and said with a smile, "That would not work either."

Morihei starred in two television documentaries. In 1958 he was featured in a segment of the United States TV series, "Rendezvous with Adventure," and in 1961 "King of Aikido" was broadcast on Japanese television. Morihei was showered with honors during his last years from both Japanese and foreign organizations, and he was decorated by the emperor in 1964. A new Hombu Dojo, ten times the size of the old one, was built in 1967. There was one thing Morihei did not like about the new dojo. Sometimes the intercom would ring, interrupting Morihei at his prayers, and he would storm out of the building, railing against such irritating modern contraptions. In the evenings, though, Morihei enjoyed watching Sumo tournaments and samurai dramas with his grandchildren on the modern contraption of television.

Morihei's Final Days

In March of 1968 Morihei collapsed in Iwama. Aware that the end was near—"The gods are calling me"—Morihei rose early on the morning of March 10 and led a training session for the last time. He was then hospitalized and his condition diagnosed as liver cancer. Morihei refused surgery and demanded to be returned home. There, as he awaited his final call, he smiled softly to himself as he heard the sounds of practice arising from the the dojo next door.

Even on his deathbed, Morihei was an invincible warrior. Just prior to his death, four of his disciples rushed to his assistance when he rose from the bed to walk to the toilet. Morihei shrugged slightly, and all four young men went flying out into the garden. On another such trip, he disappeared, and his disciples found him in the dojo teaching a bunch of children: "This is how you do it! This is how you do it!"

Near the end, Morihei told a visitor, "I'm on a winged horse floating through the clouds, gazing down on the beautiful earth below." Eighty-six-year-old Morihei quietly passed away early on the morning of April 26, 1969. Among his final words were, "Aikido is for the entire world."

PART TWO

MORIHEI UESHIBA AND THE CREATION OF AIKIDO

Early Developments, 1883–1945

Tanabe City viewed from the opposite side of the bay. Morihei's childhood home was only a few minutes from the Pacific Ocean and much of his youth was spent fishing and swimming in this bay. The climate in this part of Kii Province (present-day Wakayama Prefecture) is temperate, but on occasion violent storms blow up suddenly, churning the normally placid waters of Tanabe Bay.

The holy Kumano Mountains and the sacred Nachi Falls. The mountain mandala of Kumano marks the gateway to the divine, and it has been a mecca for pilgrims and religious seekers for millennia. One medieval pilgrim wrote in his diary: "After many days of traversing high peaks and descending through deep valleys, I finally reached the sacred land of Kumano. The journey was difficult and dangerous, and I felt fortunate in reaching my destination alive. At the main shrine, tears of joy streamed down my cheeks." Morihei said, "My spirit was nurtured by Kumano, and part of me is always there, immersed in its wondrous mountains, forests, and seas. In Kumano, I feel as if I'm walking on air." Kumano—said to contain thirty-six hundred peaks—is one of the least spoiled regions in Japan; four-fifths of the land remains undeveloped.

The Buddhist monk Mongaku undergoing *misogi* (ritual purification) in the Nachi Falls. This is an ancient religious practice, believed to cleanse both body and mind of impurities. In his early days, Morihei, too, performed misogi in the sacred Nachi Falls.

Tantric Buddhist Fire Ceremony. Morihei delighted in such spectacular ceremonies as a young man and he learned the chants, ritual gestures, and visualization techniques of Tantra well enough to be granted a "Seal of Attainment" from a Shingon Buddhist master. Morihei's worldview was always that of rich and expressive Tantra rather than that of austere and unadorned Zen.

Twenty-one-year-old Morihei (top center) as a member of the Sixty-First Wakayama Regiment, formed prior to the outbreak of the Russo-Japanese War in 1905. Morihei relished the discipline and challenge of military life—without complaint the gung-ho soldier rose an hour early each day to spit and polish thirteen pairs of boots used by his superiors, and he gladly picked up and carried along the heavy packs dropped by stragglers during forced marches—but was sorely troubled, even at that young age, by the awful death and destruction wrought by war.

Kumagusu Minakata (1867–1941) as a young man. In his twenties and thirties, Morihei had a series of "meetings with remarkable men" that shaped his destiny. The first such remarkable man was Kumagusu, eccentric scholar and environmentalist, from whom Morihei learned the importance of viewing the world as an integrated whole. Kumagusu also alerted Morihei to the dangers of mindless development and the perils of plundering natural resources. In his later years, Morihei often remarked to his disciples, "Kumagusu was a great man and he really inspired me to study hard and think about the world at large."

(*Top*) Thirty-year-old Morihei, to the right, clearing land as a pioneer in the wilds of Hokkaido. (*Bottom*) The main Shirataki settlement. In Hokkaido, Morihei greatly increased his power by wrestling the kind of large logs seen in the foreground.

Morihei sitting on the bank fishing in the Yubetsu River. In the first
years of the Shirataki settlement, crop yields were poor, and the pioneers relied heavily on fish to supplement their diet.

Formal portrait of Sokaku Takeda (1859–1943), grand master of the Daito Ryu, around the age of thirty. Note that Sokaku has assumed a combative *hanmi* stance with his feet.

(*Top*) Sokaku (right of center) with law enforcement officers at a training session conducted in 1898. Although surrounded by policemen, the ever-alert Sokaku brandishes an iron fan in his right hand, ready for any type of sneak attack. (*Bottom*) eighty-year-old Sokaku demonstrates a devastating Daito Ryu technique.

Sokaku as he appeared when Morihei first met him in Hokkaido. Sokaku's grim countenance was due to an injury he suffered as a young man. In a demonstration against three men armed with spears, Sokaku avoided their attacks and shattered one of the spears with his sword but the flying spear blade ricocheted off the ground and struck him in the mouth, knocking out most of his front teeth. Sokaku, last of the old-time warriors, was the second "remarkable man" Morihei encountered; it was Sokaku who provided Morihei with the physical forms that Morihei adapted and transformed into the techniques of Aikido.

Morihei (seated far left) and the rest of the council members of Yubetsu Village, Shirataki District, in 1918. A social activist the first
half of his life, Morihei worked with the government to promote the
welfare of citizens and, when necessary, he worked against it when
officials violated the public trust. This photograph illustrates the
transition from old to new Japan. While most of the council members
are decked out in traditional *kimono*, even at this early date in
remote Hokkaido, several members are already sporting Western-
style clothes. (Morihei, however, dressed Japanese style to the end of
his days.)

Nao Deguchi (1836–1918), mouthpiece for the god Konjin and founder of Omoto-kyo, in 1916 at age eighty.

Onisaburo Deguchi (1871–1948), the Great Guru of Omoto-kyo, turned out in shaman's robes. Onisaburo had hundreds of magnificent outfits like this, of his own design, and loved to have himself photographed as both male and female deities. Onisaburo was the third "remarkable man" Morihei encountered, the master who opened Morihei's eyes to the spiritual dimension of life. Morihei was deeply influenced in turn by Kumagusu, Sokaku, and Onisaburo, among the most creative, forceful, and eccentric geniuses of the first half of the twentieth century in Japan.

(*Left*) A dignified Onisaburo photographed in 1931 at age sixty; (*right*) a zany self-portrait. Unlike many self-proclaimed messiahs, who tend to be—quite literally—deadly serious, Onisaburo was incurably happy-go-lucky. He was a clever punster and excellent comedian who made even his enemies laugh uproariously.

(*Above*) Onisaburo, resplendent in another fantastic outfit, wielding an enormous brush to write the characters MI-ROKU-DEN. The characters were carved into wood and hung as the signboard for the Miroku Hall at the Omoto-kyo compound. (*Opposite*) *Hikari,* the character for "light," brushed by Onisaburo. Following Onisaburo's lead, Morihei often employed the image of light in Aikido, the light of wisdom that dispels darkness and despair.

Two Zen paintings by Onisaburo: (*opposite*) Bodhidharma (Daruma), the Grand Patriarch of Zen; (*above*) Zen crow. Once a Zen priest challenged Onisaburo with the well-known koan: "What is the sound of one hand clapping?" Onisaburo immediately slapped his ample belly and shot back, "Did you hear it?" Like a real Zen master, Onisaburo created his art in the here and now. Once he accidentally spilled ink over the paper he was going to use and without missing a beat, he splashed water on the paper, pulled on the sides to spread it around to create a moon surrounded by dark clouds. Zen was just one of the elements Onisaburo incorporated in his eclectic teachings.

(*Right*) Ink painting of a pine tree by Onisaburo. Instead of using a regular seal, Onisaburo stamped this piece with his thumbprint (symbolizing the sun) to activate it as a talisman, a practice akin to the Tibetan custom of having a high lama put his handprints on the back of a *thangka* to consecrate it. (*Opposite*) Two pieces of pottery created by Onisaburo. (*Top*) Chunks of this plate, smashed during the Second Omoto-kyo Incident, were secretly collected and later painstakingly pieced together. (*Bottom*) Japanese tea bowls tend to be rather somber and severe but the ones created by Onisaburo explode with bright, joyful, and vivid color. Onisaburo gave his bowls such poetic names as "Heaven's Pleasure Garden" and "Spring Deep in the Mountains."

Two images taken from 1921 when Morihei was thirty-eight years old: (*top*) Morihei seated samurai style and looking suitably formidable in front of a Daito Ryu Aiki Jujutsu signboard; (*bottom*) a more formal, less intense portrait based on a photograph taken in that year.

(*Top*) Morihei (center) in the Omoto-kyo organic gardens at Ayabe. Fresh, pesticide-free vegetables and fruit were important for the Omoto-kyo diet, and it was Morihei's job to see that the gardens were bountiful. Another of Morihei's responsibilities at Ayabe was fire-brigade leader (*bottom*). Morihei (slightly right of center facing the camera) participates in a fire drill with Onisaburo (holding the fire hose, also facing the camera) and the other Omoto-kyo fire-brigade members.

Onisaburo (second from left) and his group in Tonan at the beginning of the Great Mongolian Adventure. Photo dated March 22, 1924. The members are from left: Sasaki, Onisaburo, Okazaki, Oishi, Matsumura, Nada, and Morihei (extreme right). Onisaburo, Matsumura, Nada, and Morihei formed the core group from Omoto-kyo in Ayabe. The others were Japanese living in Manchuria, and served as translators and guides. In addition to looking for Shambhala, Omoto-kyo literature suggests that Onisaburo was additionally trying to locate Nao's lost son Kiyokichi. Nao had supposedly received word through her psychic network that Kiyokichi had not been killed in the Sino-Japanese War as reported, but had survived as a bandit king in Manchuria. Onisaburo did not find Nao's son but he did meet a bandit queen who claimed that Kiyokichi was her father and that he had died in Taiwan.

Morihei performing the chinkon-kishin meditation technique on the plains of Mongolia. Morihei, who was given the Chinese name Wang Shou-kao by Onisaburo, played the part of an Omoto-kyo lama during the adventure: praying dramatically like this, healing the sick (with his knowledge of Japanese massage and bone-setting), and performing miracles (using Jujutsu techniques to down much bigger men).

Onisaburo with two Mongolian beauties. Onisaburo reported favorably on the Mongolian nomad custom of offering guests the use of their daughters or wives for the night. One nomad tried to present Onisaburo with the gift of his fourteen-year-old daughter, a girl as "lovely as Kannon, the Goddess of Compassion." Onisaburo declined.

Onisaburo (center, wearing round hat) and Morihei (second from right) with members of Lu's army near Solun in Mongolia. Onisaburo insisted that both he and his personal guard be mounted on white horses, a privilege normally reserved for kings and emperors. Onisaburo liked to make a grand entrance mounted on a snow white steed but he was in fact a poor horseman, injuring himself quite badly in several serious falls. Morihei was a more skilled rider thanks to his days in Hokkaido but he was, of course, no match for the Mongols, who are practically raised on horseback.

As Onisaburo and his group approached Paiyintala in early June 1924, it dawned on the Omoto-kyo Grand Lama that Lu and his men were in big trouble. The Chinese army was closing in and their caravan had been under constant attack the past few weeks by bandits. Onisaburo, Matsumura, and Morihei secluded themselves in a cave to fast and pray for guidance. That night Onisaburo received the bad news: Lu and his party were heading straight into a lion's den.

Onisaburo attempted to dissuade Lu from entering the city but when the bandit chief insisted, Onisaburo, Matsumura, and Morihei (the three small figures in the upper left) made a final supplication to the gods from the top of a hill and went to meet their fate.

June 30, 1924, at the Paiyintala Prison. Captured by the Chinese army, bound in leg irons, and marched to the execution ground: (from left) Matsumura, Onisaburo, Morihei, Ogiwara, Inoue, and Sakamoto. Other than serving as group photographer, Ogiwara's role is not clear; Inoue and Sakamoto were well-known agents provocateurs who could have been executed with justification as spies and espionage agents.

Onisaburo, Morihei (far right), and the rest of the group on the boat back to Japan. They arrived in Japan on July 25, 1924. Onisaburo was immediately arrested for violation of the conditions of his bail bond.

Morihei in pilgrim garb in front of the Nachi Falls around
1925. Following his return to Japan after the Great Mongolian Adventure, Morihei intensified his training in Budo and
returned to the mountains of Kumano for ascetic practice.

SHAMBHALA

The sun
in the form of a falcon,
the Book of the Dead of
Hunefer, British Museum,
from *The Myth of Isis and Osiris*
(Shambhala, 1994)

SHAMBHALA

If you wish to receive a copy of the latest Shambhala Publications catalogue of books and to be placed on our mailing list please send us this card.

Please print

BOOK IN WHICH THIS CARD WAS FOUND ....

NAME ....

ADDRESS ....

CITY .... STATE ....

ZIP OR POSTAL CODE ....

COUNTRY (*if outside U.S.A.*) ....

Detach bookmark before mailing card.

SHAMBHALA

SHAMBHALA PUBLICATIONS, INC.

MAILING LIST

P.O. BOX 308, BACK BAY ANNEX

BOSTON, MASSACHUSETTS   02117-0308

The sacred woods behind the Omoto-kyo compound in Ayabe where Morihei trained at night. (The houses in the foreground are recent additions.) When Morihei was practicing there, Omoto-kyo members below heard strange sounds and felt chill breezes emanating from the woods. Today, these woods are off-limits for all but a few Omoto-kyo officials.

Morihei at forty-two, the age at which he experienced Great Awakening. The fantastic ascending dragon (brushed by Onisaburo?) in the background symbolizes Morihei's soaring spirit at this time.

Morihei in 1925 with his sole surviving son, Kisshomaru. In 1927, Morihei and his family left Ayabe to settle in Tokyo.

Morihei demonstrating at the opening of the Kobukan in March of 1931.

A formal portrait of the dignitaries attending the opening ceremony of the Kobukan. Morihei (center) is surrounded by military elite, important government officials, wealthy businessmen, well-known physicians, and other dignitaries. The signboard to the right of the alcove, brushed by Onisaburo, reads "Ueshiba Juku" (Ueshiba Academy).

(*Top*) Morihei with Hidemaru and Naohi Deguchi seated in the place of honor. Morihei was quite close to Hidemaru (Onisaburo's son-in-law), and most of the calligraphy displayed here in the Kobukan was brushed by Hidemaru. During the Second Omoto-kyo Incident, Hidemaru was tortured so severely that he went insane and only partly recovered after the war. The signboard placed to the left of the alcove appears to be a Daito Ryu certificate of some type. It was not displayed during the opening ceremony of the Kobukan, and quickly disappeared from the dojo wall. (*Bottom*) Photo taken at a dojo celebration with the live-in disciples and a few supporters.

A less formal group shot of Morihei and Hidemaru (seated to the right of Morihei in a white *hakama*) with the Kobukan trainees.

Although Onisaburo was Morihei's root guru, he was also influenced by the teachings of Bonji Kawatsura (1862–1929). In his early twenties Kawatsura secluded himself in the mountains of Usa, where he encountered a wizard, reputed to be 697 years old, who imparted various secret teachings to Kawatsura. Kawatsura also studied Buddhism and then went on to found the Misogi Kai. Kawatsura is responsible for reviving and popularizing the ancient practice of *misogi-no-gyo*, ritual purification. Many of the warm-up exercises employed in Aikido (such as *tori-fune undo*, "rowing the boat") are derived from Kawatsura's version of misogi-no-gyo.

Morihei, around age fifty, at his physical peak. In the prewar period, the hard-edged martial aspect of his character was dominant—severe, solid, and intent.

Morihei standing next to Sumi and Onisaburo Deguchi in front of the banner for the Dainihon Budo Senyo Kai, an organization set up in 1932 by Onisaburo and Morihei to promote Morihei's Omoto-kyo-flavored Aiki Budo. The Budo Senyo Kai was loosely organized along paramilitary lines, hence the uniforms. This is one of the few occasions on which Morihei appeared in Western dress (sporting a bow tie, no less).

An interesting shot of Morihei and his wife, Hatsu, with a group of
Omoto-kyo believers in the shrine room of an Omoto-kyo family.
Since several of Morihei's disciples can be seen in the photo, it was
likely taken after a training session sponsored by the Budo Senyo Kai.

The Budo Senyo Kai had a boot camp in Takeda. Every summer Morihei (back row center) and his top students would gather there for intensive training. Among the trainees pictured here are: Kiyoshi Nakakura (standing, far left), Morihei's one-time son-in-law and the greatest Kendo man of the modern era; Rinjiro Shirata (seated front row, second from the left), the "Flower of the Kobukan," perhaps the most talented of Morihei's prewar disciples; Tsutomu Yukawa (to the right of Shirata), nicknamed "Samson" due to his prodigious strength; Gozo Shioda (to the right of Morihei, wearing glasses), founder of Yoshinkan Aikido; Kisshomaru Ueshiba (behind Shioda), Morihei's son and eventual successor; and Kenji Tomiki and Yoichiro Inoue (back row, third and fourth from the right), founders, respectively, of Tomiki Ryu Aikido and Shinwa Taido. Mrs. Ueshiba is to the right of Shioda.

Scenes from various Aiki Budo seminars. Some seminars consisted of a formal demonstration and lecture before assembled dignitaries (*above*) while others were actually training sessions (*overleaf*). The fee for these seminars was rather high and participation was generally by invitation only.

Morihei and Rinjiro Shirata (to Morihei's right) at the Ichi-ku Kai dojo. The Ichi-ku Kai was established by Tetsuju Ogura, a top disciple of the Zen Master and Muto Ryu swordsman Tesshu Yamaoka. (Portraits of the two men are hanging on the wall; Tetsuju to the left, and Tesshu to the right.) Both before and after the war, a number of Morihei's disciples practiced Zen meditation and misogi chanting at the Ichi-ku Kai.

Two formal portraits of Morihei at age fifty-two, one made with a camera and one painted by Takako Kunigoshi. (The crest on the kimono is that of Omoto-kyo.) At the Kobukan, the spirited Miss Kunigoshi trained on the same basis as the men, asking for and giving no quarter—she was frequently called on by Morihei to demonstrate the efficacy of Aiki Budo techniques against male attackers. Miss Kunigoshi was a talented amateur artist as well and she did this portrait of Morihei in 1935.

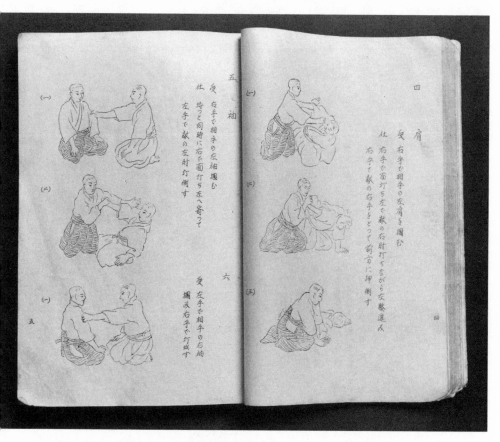

Miss Kunigoshi drew the illustrations for *Budo Renshu,* an instruction manual by Morihei, privately published in 1933.

Morihei giving pointers on swordsmanship to a group of classical Japanese dancers. Classical dance instructors and Kabuki actors frequently sought Morihei's advice on martial art movements. One day a noted classical Japanese dance teacher visited the Kobukan to request instruction in the *naginata* (halberd). Morihei hesitated a bit because he had little experience with that particular weapon, which is mainly used by females. Charmed, however, by the lovely teacher, he consented. Morihei ordered a disciple to obtain a popular novel in which the hero is a master of naginata, place the book on the Shinto altar, and see that he not be disturbed for the remainder of the day.

When the dance instructor returned for her lesson, Morihei showed her a series of beautiful moves. Later, after the woman had performed them on stage, she was told by a surprised naginata master, "What wonderful techniques! Where did you learn them?"

His puzzled disciples asked Morihei how he was able to master the naginata so quickly. "The hero of the novel visited me while I was in a trance and taught me his secrets," was the reply.

Spooky Shojobo Valley on Mount Kurama, abode of the tengu who impart the secrets of Budo to worthy warriors. Once a year, Morihei took several of his best disciples to train with him on Mount Kurama, located near Kyoto. The small group lived on rice, pickles, miso soup, and wild herbs. Morihei would rise at five o'clock in the morning to pray. After morning prayers and misogi, they would swing heavy swords five hundred times and then practice footwork. From ten o'clock to noon they trained in body techniques. Afternoon training ran from three to five o'clock; the disciples took turns acting as Morihei's partner as he ran through series after series of techniques. In the evening the disciples would review the day's training. Every three days, Morihei would announce at midnight, "Time for night training." The disciples could discern nothing in the pitch-darkness, but Morihei cried out to them, "Watch out for the rock on your left! Duck to avoid the upcoming branches!" He armed them with wooden swords and commanded them to attack. At first, none of the disciples had the slightest notion where their teacher was; gradually, however, they sensed his presence to the right or left and sped up their attacks. Then Morihei turned the tables: he chased after them, bringing his razor-sharp blade within a hair's breadth of their headbands.

The tengu king Shojobo imparting the secrets of Budo to Ushiwaka-maru on Mount Kurama. This has been a favorite theme of Japanese artists through the centuries. Morihei would take his favorite students to Mount Kurama and tell them, "This is the spot where Ushiwakamaru learned from Shojobo!"

Morihei, his wife Hatsu, his son Kisshomaru,
and a niece, in Tokyo in 1938 or 1939.

Morihei with Kenji Tomiki (seated next to Morihei), Hideo Oba (standing behind Morihei) and an unidentified student, in Manchuria, August 1942. Morihei was closely associated with Kenkoku University in Manchuria, serving as Professor of Martial Arts. During an important demonstration, Oba threw all caution to the wind and attacked Morihei as if he were trying to kill him. Although Oba's determination to make the demonstration realistic was admirable, it was also foolhardy since full-force attacks have to be countered full-force, and that can be lethal. Morihei was furious with Oba for playing with fire, but after the demonstration the other martial art instructors present—the cream of the crop—praised Morihei's techniques as the "real thing."

Morihei back home in Tanabe: by the bay (*above*); next to his ancestral home (*left*); and in front of a neighborhood shrine (*right*). These photos were evidently taken in the early 1940s, perhaps just before Morihei resigned all of his official positions and went to Iwama.

In 1942 Morihei left his son Kisshomaru in charge of the Kobukan in Tokyo and he and his wife moved to Iwama to live in this little hut. Here, during one of the darkest periods in human history, Morihei vowed to devote his life to his new art of Aikido, the Way of Harmony and Peace.

Grand Master of Aikido, 1946–1969

Morihei at age fifty-three (*top*) and at age sixty-eight (*bottom*). After the war Morihei assumed the countenance and demeanor of a Taoist immortal of great and indeterminate age.

Although most postwar photographs show Morihei smiling happily, a few capture him in his manifestation as a god of righteous anger. A terrifying glare such as this could freeze anyone in his or her tracks and send a chill through the spine. When Morihei exploded in anger, the rafters shook, his brave disciples cowered in a corner, and people in the neighborhood ran for cover. Morihei never struck anyone in anger, of course, but he didn't need to; his wrath was so dreadful that anyone scolded by him trembled for days afterward. After the outburst, Morihei's normally sunny disposition would return. "It is all over now," he would reassure his terrified disciples. "It was only the wrathful gods that were displeased with you."

Morihei devoted much of his time at Iwama to creating an Aiki Shrine (*top*). Morihei's Aiki Shrine was dedicated to the forty-two guardian deities of the universe, each personifying one of the elemental forces that activate and sustain the cosmos—for example, energy, light, water, fire, and, of course, love. The Aiki Shrine embodies the ideals of Aikido, and Morihei worshiped there every morning (*bottom*).

In 1962 Morihei had a larger Aiki Shrine constructed. Here he conducts a purification ceremony to commemorate the raising of the shrine roof.

(*Top*) The completed shrine and *torii*. (*Bottom*) Interior of the main Aiki Shrine. The Shinto altar, graced with offerings of fresh vegetables and rice wine, is Omoto-kyo style. The calligraphy displayed on the sides announces the names of two Omoto-kyo deities: *Hitsuji-saru-Kimon-Dai-Konsei* (*left*) and *Ushitora-Kimon-Dai-Konsei* (*right*). Every year on April 29, a Shinto ceremony is held at the Aiki Shrine in memory of Morihei's spirit.

Morihei in 1952, age sixty-eight. In the 1950s a second "golden age" began as a new crop of trainees took up practice of the revolutionary new art of Aikido.

Morihei, age seventy-eight, and his son Kisshomaru, age thirty-seven, in 1958. After the war, the Aiki Kai (Aiki Foundation) was formed to promote Aikido at home and abroad; the Kobukan was renamed Hombu Dojo (Headquarters Dojo).

A delighted Morihei receiving a traditional Hawaiian greeting on his trip to the islands in 1961. He made the trip "to build a silver bridge" between Japan and other countries of the world. Morihei's calligraphy, *Masakatsu Agatsu Katsuhayabi* ("True Victory is Self-Victory. Right Here, Right Now!") hangs in the alcove.

Morihei in a Hawaiian dojo. His calligraphy *Ame-no-mu-rakumo Kuki Samuhara Su Okami/Katsuhayabi Tenkoka* ("The Great Deity Ame no Murakumo Kuki Samuhara/Now Triumphant and Incarnate Among Us") hangs in the background.

(*Above*) Memorial photograph taken after the dedication ceremony for the Honolulu Aiki dojo on March 11, 1961. Koichi Tohei, the father of Aikido in the United States, sits to Morihei's left. (*Opposite*) Morihei conducting a seminar with Nobuyoshi Tamura as his partner. Morihei stayed in Hawaii for forty days. He said, "People could not understand what I was saying but they could understand Aikido by the way I acted and moved. Aikido is a heart-to-heart transmission not dependent on words."

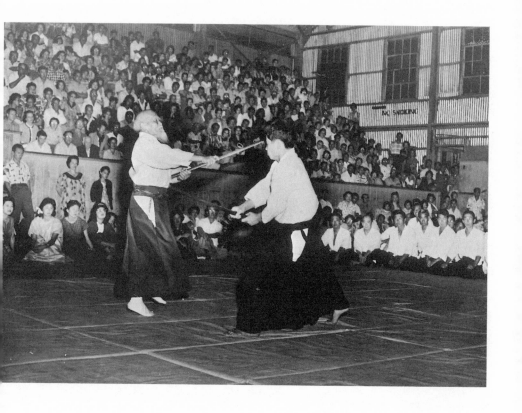

Morihei relaxing in the garden of the
Royal Hawaiian Hotel, a Honolulu landmark.

Morihei praying for world peace on the island of Maui.

(*Top*) Group shot of Morihei and Hombu Dojo instructors and trainees taken in the early 1960s. (*Bottom*) Morihei and his wife, Morihiro Saito and his wife, and a group of college students in front of Iwama dojo, around 1965.

In his mature years, Morihei would pray, meditate, and study when he was not training. His favorite texts for study were Onisaburo's *Reiki Monogatari,* the *Kojiki,* and the *Nihon Shoki.*

(*Opposite*) When Morihei led the training, he would typically discourse on the profundities of Aikido for thirty minutes or more, often acting out various principles with body movements. (*Above*) On occasion, Morihei would give more formal lectures. Here he explains the symbolism of the subtle wisdom-body all human beings possess.

たちからをのみこと
多力雄の命

Morihei spoke in a kind of code language, replete with symbolic tales taken from Shinto mythology, Tantric cosmology, and Omoto-kyo doctrine. He believed that he was a direct ancestor of the Shinto Hercules Tachikara-o (*above*) and an incarnation of the Dragon King Ame-no-murakumo Kuki Samuhara Ryu-o (*opposite*) depicted in the hanging scroll behind Morihei.

Morihei enjoyed brushing calligraphy to present to his disciples, supporters, and friends. (*Above*) Morihei in the Hombu Dojo brushing "Masakatsu Agatsu"; (*below*), Morihei explains the significance of a piece of calligraphy (*Ame-no-murakumo Kuki Samuhara Ryu-o Okami*) presented to a friend.

The Chinese character for ki, "life force." It is signed
"Tsunemori," a pen name used by Morihei in his seventies.

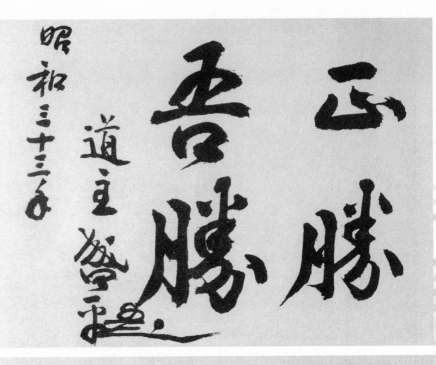

Masakatsu Agatsu, "True victory is victory over oneself," (*top*) and *Katsuhayabi*, "Victory right here, right now" (*bottom*). Both pieces are dated 1958 and signed "Grand Master Morihei." The piece at the bottom has aiki added to the signature.

"Ko-shin" (also read *"Hikari-no-kami"*), "Light Divine." Morihei often termed Aikido the "Path of Light."

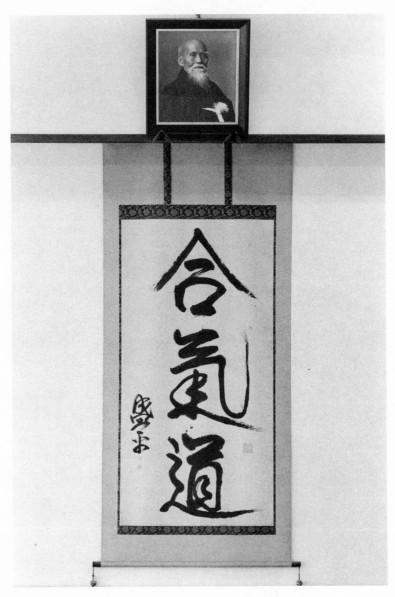

"Aikido," the scroll hung in the main training hall of the Hombu Dojo.

Morihei at the first public demonstration of Aikido, in 1956. Previously, Morihei (like all the old-time masters) had been adamantly opposed to open performances lest his techniques be stolen and misused by unsavory characters. Another initial objection made by Morihei is that only the grand master is qualified to demonstrate; his disciples are still being trained and onlookers may get the wrong impression if they witness half-baked Aikido performed by novices. He reluctantly agreed to this performance after Kisshomaru pleaded with him to do so for the spread of Aikido. Morihei turned out to have enjoyed this experience, realized the value of such demonstrations (as a celebration of Aikido), and let himself be freely photographed and filmed. (Except, on occasion, at Iwama. There were many yakuza in the town, and Morihei canceled several public demonstrations at the Aiki Shrine because of the presence of gangsters.)

Morihei greeting United States astronaut John Glenn (left) and his son in 1963. Through an interpreter, Morihei amazed Glenn with his detailed knowledge of outer space; it seemed as if Morihei had toured the heavens himself.

Morihei kept his contacts with Omoto-kyo after the war (*above*, sitting with Naohi Deguchi) and he enjoyed meeting other spiritual teachers such as Masatoshi Doi (*opposite top*), head of the Byakko Prayer Society. Morihei also continued to associate with teachers of classical Japanese dance (*opposite bottom*).

Morihei always enjoyed returning to Iwama to farm and garden (*above*) and to train in the woods (*opposite*).

Morihei with his devoted wife, Hatsu, in scenes from before (*above*) and after the war (*opposite*). One of Morihei's disciples once remarked that "without Mrs. Ueshiba, Aikido would never have been created." She ran the household for her mercurial husband, prepared the simple home-cooked meals he savored—no red meat, some chicken and fish, lots of vegetables including, yes, spinach—and tolerated his many idiosyncrasies. Whenever Morihei accidentally ripped his kimono in a demonstration, he would joke, "I'm in trouble now. Grandma will really scold me for this." Hatsu died two months to the day after Morihei.

Morihei, age seventy-nine. In most photographs taken of
Morihei in his later years, he appears to be gazing far into
the distance, his sights fixed on things not of this mundane
world.

Near the end of his life, Morihei
assumed an ethereal, almost
phantom-like presence.

Even though his physical form was fading away, Morihei retained the amazing powers of an invincible warrior.

Several times in his final years Morihei sadly reflected, "I've given my life to opening the path of Aikido but when I look back no one is following me." Once an American disciple said to Morihei, "I really want to do your Aikido." Morihei replied, "How unusual! Everyone else wants to do their own Aikido."

Until just before the end, Morihei was on the mat, continually refining his Aikido.

Morihei in the final year of his life, 1969.

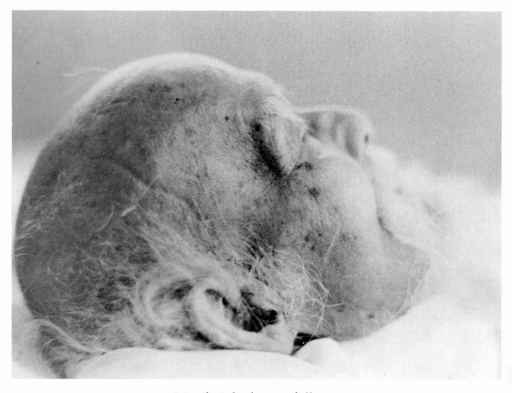

Morihei died peacefully,
early in the morning of April 26, 1969, age eighty-six.

(*Top*) Morihei's tomb is located on the grounds of Takayama-dera, a Buddhist temple in Tanabe; (*bottom*), memorial statue of Morihei erected in Tanabe City.

PART THREE

THE MARVELOUS TECHNIQUES OF MORIHEI UESHIBA

Morihei's techniques are usually divided into two distinct phases: prewar Aiki Budo techniques and postwar Aikido techniques. Regarding the techniques of Aiki Budo, Morihei stated that they "gushed forth like a spring." Admiral Takeshita, one of Morihei's most devoted prewar students, made a record of every technique he learned from Morihei over a two-year period: there were 10,987 techniques recorded in his twenty-two-volume training diary. Morihei's prewar techniques were recorded on film in a movie shot in Osaka in 1935; in two teaching manuals, *Budo Renshu* (1933) and *Budo* (1938); and in a series of photographs shot at the Noma Dojo (1936). The selection of prewar Aiki Budo techniques that follows consists of previously unpublished photographs taken from the Noma Dojo series and unpublished excerpts from *Budo*.

Regarding the transformation of Aiki Budo techniques into Aikido techniques, Morihei related this experience: "On December 14, 1940, I was performing ritual purification around two o'clock in the morning when I suddenly forgot every martial art technique I had ever learned. All of the techniques handed down to me from my teachers appeared completely anew. Now my techniques were vehicles for the cultivation of life, knowledge, virtue, and good sense, not mere devices to throw and pin people." Morihei also stated, "Before the war, my techniques were all power and physical force, but then I realized that such a waste of energy is not necessary. If you can walk, you have enough *ki* (vital life force) to down your partner; if you have the strength to open a door, you can practice Aikido." No formal instruction manuals were produced by Morihei in the postwar years; the illustrations presented here are taken from existing photographs and grouped together.

Actually, the distinction between Aiki Budo and Aikido techniques should not be overstressed since there is, in fact, a definite continuity between the prewar and postwar forms, as can be seen in the accompanying illustrations. In general, the main difference is that Morihei's postwar Aikido techniques tended to be more circular, less complex technically, and executed with a lighter touch.

Prewar Aiki Budo Techniques

Shiho-nage Variations

—— 1 ——

—— 2 ——

Irimi-nage Variations

—— 1 ——

—— 3 ——

—— 4 ——

—— 5 ——

— 6 —

—— 7 ——

—— 8 ——

—— 9 ——

—— 10 ——

—— 12 ——

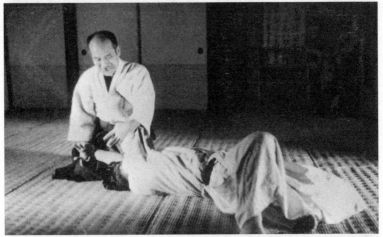

— 2 —

Kokyu-nage Variations

— 3 —

— 4 —

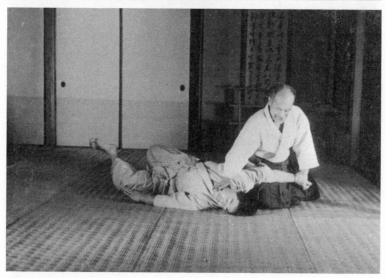

—— 7 ——

— 8 —

— 9 —

—— 10 ——

Pin Variations

—— 2 ——

— 3 —

— 4 —

— 5 —

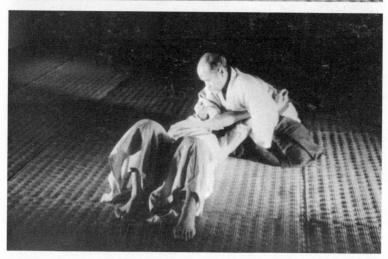

—— 9 ——

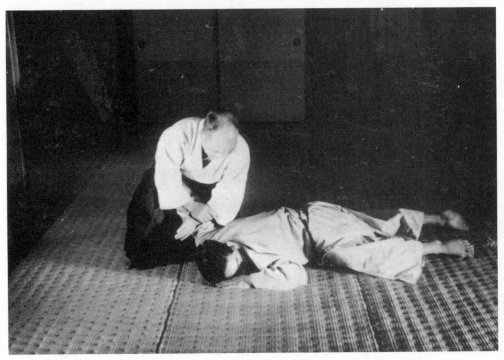

— 10 —

Kubi-nage Variations

— 2 —

—— 3 ——

— 4 —

—— 5 ——

—— 6 ——

— 7 —

Hip-Throw Variations

— 1 —

—— 2 ——

—— 3 ——

—— 4 ——

Tenchi-nage Variations

—— 1 ——

—— 2 ——

Ushiro Technique Variations
—— 1 ——

—— 2 ——

Smiling Technique Variations

—— 1 ——

—— 2 ——

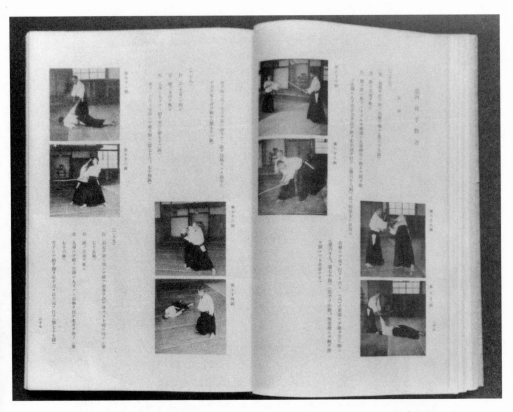

The original edition of *Budo,* which cost the equivalent of $200. The photographs used for this edition are long gone but some outtakes remain; the shots that follow are the only ones that have not been published in the author's other books.

Suwari Kokyu-ho

—— 1 ——

—— 2 ——

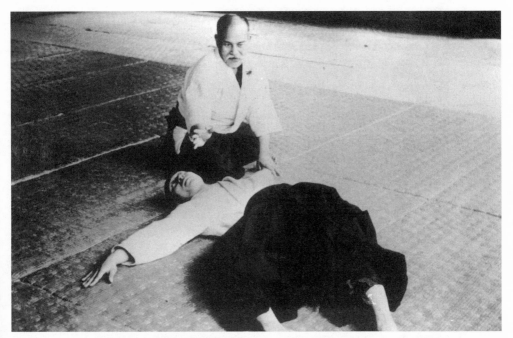

Morihei demonstrating the proper method of holding a spear.

Irimi movement applied against sword attack.

Irimi-nage.

Kote-gaeshi.

Ikkyo pin.

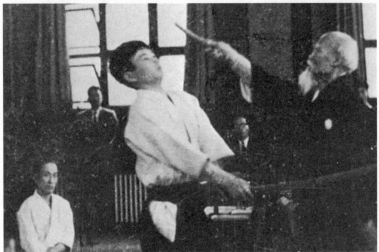

In his later years, Morihei maintained that "Aikido has no techniques." Here he demonstrates the no-sword technique and the stance of no-stance. (*Top*) Morihei, with his body turned slightly to the right, is perfectly poised, and his softly focused gaze envelopes his armed opponent. His stance is solid but not at all static—it is one hundred percent natural, and he seems to be inviting the swordsman to strike. Morihei displays here *fudo-shin*, "an immovable mind," which can respond to any contingency without a loss of composure. (*Bottom*) As soon as the attack commences, Morihei moves in with *irimi* directly toward his opponent's vital spots with just the right amount of movement—neither too fast nor too slow: "There is no time and space in Aikido—the techniques must arise right where you are."

The principle of irimi, entering deeply, physically, and spiritually, remained a key element in both pre- and postwar techniques. _____

Irimi-nage

Kaiten

Kaiten, "body turn" is applicable against one partner (*above*) or many (*opposite*), is often thought of as the most fundamental Aikido technique, yet it is the one that Morihei demonstrated when he was asked by an inquisitive reporter, "What is the ultimate Aikido technique?" "That's it?" the puzzled reporter said. "Yes, that's it," Morihei replied with a smile.

Kokyu-ho

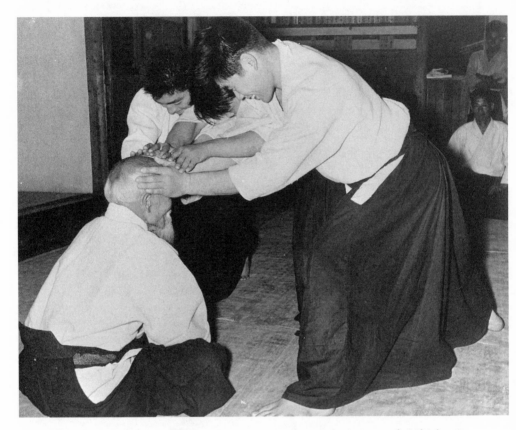

Kokyu-ho, "breath power," animates the techniques of Aikido. It can make one an immovable object (*above*) or an irresistible force (*opposite*).

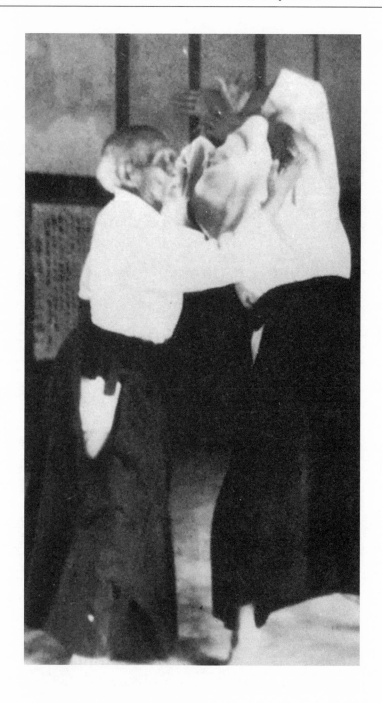

Kokyu-nage

Standing.

Seated.

Morihei taught, "learn how to walk correctly and you can master Aikido." Many Aikido techniques such as *kokyu-nage* (*top*) and *ikkyo* (*bottom*) are based on natural walking movements.

In the postwar years, Morihei began every training session with misogi-no-jo to restore his link to the divine and to purify the dojo. Misogi-no-jo is a sacred dance, performed with a four-foot staff, that puts one in the proper state of mind to practice Aikido. The signboard above Morihei reads, "Outside of the mind there is no Dharma."

Morihei and Kisshomaru practicing *kumi-jo*, paired jo exercises. Morihei taught that jo training fosters intuition and facilitates understanding of the principle of entering.

(*Above*) Morihei practicing *tanren-uchi,* "chopping wood with a sword," to strengthen the hands, shoulders, and hips. (*Opposite*) Morihei and Kisshomaru practicing *kumi-tachi,* paired sword techniques. Most Aikido body techniques are defined in terms of sword movements.

Both before (*left*) and after (*right*) the war, Morihei stressed entering at a ninety-degree angle to counter an attack.

1936

The distinction between prewar and post-war techniques should not be overemphasized. The basic movements and core techniques remained essentially the same as we can see here in these photographs, taken thirty years apart.

circa 1966

1936

circa 1966

It may be argued that all masters end up practicing Aikido—the art of perfect timing and concentrated power. For example, superficially the techniques and training methods of Aikido and Judo appear to be quite different but when we compare the throws of Morihei and Judo master Kyuzo Mifune (1883–1965), the techniques look almost identical.

Map of Japan showing important locations in the life of Morihei Ueshiba.

Bibliography

Source Material on the Life of Morihei Ueshiba

Kisshomaru Ueshiba, Morihei's son and successor, has published a number of books in Japanese dealing with Morihei's career:

Aikido, by Kisshomaru Ueshiba under the direction of Morihei Ueshiba, was first published in 1956. A reprint edition was issued in 1996 by Shuppan Geijutsusha. This book contains an interesting interview with Morihei in which he discusses his life and the creation of Aikido.

Aikido Kaiso Ueshiba Morihei Den (Founder of Aikido: The Biography of Morihei Ueshiba) was published in 1977 by Kodansha. Now out of print and in need of some revision.

Aikido Kaiso (Founder of Aikido) is an illustrated biography published in 1983 by Kodansha to mark the 100th anniversary of Morihei's birth.

Aikido Shintai (The Truth of Aikido), a lavish coffee-table book also published by Kodansha which appeared in 1986.

Aikido Ichiro (My Life in Aikido), Kisshomaru Ueshiba's memoirs, published in 1996 by Shuppan Geijutsusha. Includes an interview with the Sumo wrestler Tenryu describing his training with Morihei on Mount Kuruma, and a group interview with Morihei's top prewar disciples.

In addition, over the last decade a number of illustrated and freshly researched articles on Morihei and the history of Aikido by K. Ueshiba and others have appeared in the magazine *Aikido Tankyu (Aikido Research),* issued annually by Geijutsu Shuppansha. Further historical material on Morihei by K. Ueshiba and others appeared in the Japanese-language journal *Aikido Magazine,* which is no longer being published. Over the past twenty years, many articles on Morihei by K. Ueshiba and others have appeared in the *Aikido Shimbun (Aikido Newspaper)* published monthly by the Aikido Headquarters in Tokyo.

Two collections of transcripts of Morihei's talks, both containing autobiographical material, have been published in Japanese: *Takemusu Aiki* (Byakko-kai, Tokyo, 1976) and *Aiki Shinzui* (Hakujusha, 1990). There are also transcripts of several radio interviews given by Morihei; particularly valuable is the NHK interview recorded on July 6, 1962. The two books Morihei published before the war, *Budo Renshu* (1933) and *Budo* (1938), are available in English translation (see Bibliography). There is a biography of Morihei titled *Bu no Shinjin (True Man of Martial Valor),* by Kanemoto Sunadomari (Tama Publishing Company, Tokyo, 1969). This is the only biography written while Morihei was still alive, and it interprets Morihei's life in light of Omoto-kyo teachings. For a detailed presentation of Morihei's Aikido philosophy see *The Essence of Aikido: Spiritual Teachings of Morihei Ueshiba,* compiled by John Stevens (Kodansha International, 1993), and *The Secrets of Aikido,* by John Stevens (Shambhala Publications, 1995).

An article on Morihei's study of Goto-ha Yagyu (Shingan) Ryu Jujutsu appeared in the Spring 1997 issue of *Gokui* magazine, published by Fukusho-do in Tokyo. The primary source of information on the career of Sokaku Takeda is his son and successor, Tokimune Takeda. A long chapter on Sokaku and the Daito-Ryu appears in *Hiden Nihon Jujutsu (Secret Transmission of Japanese Jujutsu)* edited by Ryuchi Matsuda, published by Shinjinbutsu-juraisha in 1977. A great deal of information on Sokaku regularly appears in the journal *Hiden (Secret Transmission)*, published in Tokyo. Morihei's break from Sokaku and the Daito-Ryu is described in *Aikijujutsu no Shinzui (Essence of Aikijujutsu)*, published by BAB Japan in 1996. An article that touches on the uneasy relationship between Sokaku and Morihei appeared in the May 15, 1956, issue of *Shukan Yomuri*. (This article also contains a lengthy interview with Morihei, in which he talks about his early life and prewar years. It also states that during Morihei's demonstration before the Imperial Household in 1941, Yukawa attacked Morihei with a knife Yukawa had secretly hidden on his person.) *Takeda Sokaku to Daito Ryu Aikijujutsu (Sokaku Takeda and the Daito Ryu Aikijujutsu)* was published by the *Aiki News* in 1992. A conflicting view of the relationship between Sokaku and Morihei is found in *Tomeina Chikara: Fuseishutsu no Bujutsuka—Segawa Yukiyoshi (Transparent Power: The Extraordinary Martial Artist Yukiyoshi Segawa)*, by Tatsuo Kimura (Kodansha, 1995). Segawa contends—indeed contradicts—just about every other account of Sokaku's teaching methods and the history of Daito Ryu and disparages Morihei's accomplishments. Morihei's relationship with Jigoro Kano, founder of Kodokan Judo, and Gichin Funakoshi, father of modern karate, is described in *Three Budo Masters* by John Stevens (Kodansha International, 1995).

Much information on Nao and Onisaburo Deguchi, the Budo Senyo Kai, and so on, appears in *Omoto-kyo Shichi-junen Shi (Seventy Years of Omoto-kyo History)* published by Aizen in 1989. *Oni Moko Nyuki (Onisaburo's Account of the Great Mongolian Adventure)*, first released in 1924 and reprinted by Aizen in 1994, contains several photographs and frequent references to Morihei. An English-language biography of Onisaburo, *The Great Onisaburo Deguchi,* by Kyo-taro Deguchi was published in 1973 by the Omoto-kyo Foundation.

Gozo Shioda, one of Morihei's top prewar disciples, wrote two books giving eyewitness accounts of many of Morihei's most amazing feats: *Aikido Jinsei (My Life in Aikido)* and *Aikido Shugyo (Training in Aikido),* both published by Takeuchi Shoten (1985 and 1991, respectively). Another prominent prewar disciple, Minoru Mochizuki, describes Morihei's prowess in *Do to Sen o Wasureta Nihon Budo ni Katsu (A Loud Rejoinder to All Japanese Martial Artists Who Have Lost the Way!),* published by BAB Japan in 1995. Takuo Takaoka's account of his training with Morihei in Wakayama is found in *Ki no Myojutsu (The Wonders of Ki),* by Kozo Kaku (Shuppan Geijutsusha, 1996). Yuzo Seino re-lates his studies with Morihei in *Aiki no Michi to Ningen Joken (Aikido and Humanity),* volumes I and II (Jimpo Shup-pankai, 1994). Masato Sasaki describes his experiences with Morihei in a video called *Bushin Ichido (Budo and Shinto Are One),* released in 1993 by BAB Japan. *Aikido no Kokoro o Matomete (Searching for the Heart of Aikido),* by Kanshu Sunatomari (Kanemoto's brother) and published by Gakuto-shu in 1981, contains many photographs of Morihei and de-scribes the author's experiences with the master. Interviews with most of Morihei's closest disciples have appeared over the years in *Aiki News* (now *Aiki Journal*), published in Tokyo. Many of these interviews have been collected in two volumes: *Ueshiba Morihei to Aikido (Morihei Ueshiba and Aikido)* and *Zoku Ueshiba Morihei to Aikido (More on Morihei Ueshiba and Aikido),* published by *Aiki News* in 1990 and 1994, respectively. One volume of these interviews has appeared in English translation as *Aikido Masters* (1994). In 1996, *Aiki News* published *Aikido: Heart & Sword* by Andre Nocquet, Morihei's first postwar foreign dis-ciple; the book contains many memorable photographs of Morihei taken when he was in his seventies. *Aiki News* has also produced a six-volume *Video Biography of Morihei Ueshiba,* which includes snippets of Morihei speaking. Volume 1 contains most of the demonstration film of Aiki Budo shot in 1935; volume three contains the complete United States television documentary, "Rendezvous with Adventure," filmed in 1958; and volume 6 contains the Japanese television documentary, "King of Aikido," shot in 1961. A research article titled "Martial Arts Diary by Isamu Takeshita and Morihei Ueshiba in about 1926," by Fumiaki Shishida appeared in *Budo Gaku Kenkyu (Budo Studies Research Journal),* volume 2, 1992. *Aikido in America,* by John Stone and Ron Meyer, published by Frog, Ltd., in 1995, contains interesting reminiscences of Morihei by some of his early American disciples. More such reminiscences are found in *It's a Lot Like Dancing,* by Terry Dobson, Rikki Moss, and Jan Watson (Frog, Ltd., 1994). Interviews with some of Morihei's Japanese and foreign disciples have recently appeared in *Aikido Today Magazine,* published in Claremont, California (issue 43 contains an article by Kazuaki Tanahashi, "Years Before Pearl Harbor," that describes Morihei's secret campaign to help Japan avoid war with the United States).

In addition to the above published accounts, I have made extensive use of the vast oral history that exists, collecting valuable material from public forums and countless private discussions with many of Morihei's senior disciples. Particularly informative have been discussions with Rinjiro Shirata, Kisshomaru Ueshiba, Morihiro Saito, Satoshi Okazaki, Masaichiro Daiguji, Takuo Takaoka, and Takaji Ishida.

Select Bibliography of English-Language Publications on Aikido

Dobson, Terry, Rikki Moss, and Jan Watson. *It's a Lot Like Dancing.* Berkeley, Calif.: Frog, Ltd., 1994.
Heckler, Richard. *Aikido and the New Warrior.* Berkeley, Calif.: North Atlantic Books, 1985.

Homma, Gaku. *Aikido for Life*. Berkeley, Calif.: Frog, Ltd., 1990.

O'Conner, Greg. *The Aikido Student Handbook*. Berkeley, Calif.: Frog, Ltd., 1993.

Pranin, Stanley (ed.). *Aikido Masters*. Tokyo: Aiki News, 1994.

Saotome, Mitsugi. *The Principles of Aikido*. Boston: Shambhala Publications, 1990.

———. *Aikido and the Harmony of Nature*. Boston: Shambhala Publications, 1993.

Shimizu, Kenji. *Aikido: The Heavenly Road*. Chicago: Editions q, Inc., 1994.

Shioda, Gozo. *Dynamic Aikido*. Tokyo: Kodansha International, 1968.

Stevens, John, under the direction of Rinjiro Shirata. *Aikido: The Way of Harmony*. Boston: Shambhala Publications, 1984.

Stevens, John. *The Essence of Aikido: Spiritual Teachings of Morihei Ueshiba*. Tokyo: Kodansha International, 1993.

———. *Three Budo Masters: Kano, Funakoshi, Ueshiba*. Tokyo: Kodansha International, 1995.

———. *The Secrets of Aikido*. Boston: Shambhala Publications, 1995.

———. *The Shambhala Guide to Aikido*. Boston: Shambhala Publications, 1996.

Stone, John, and Ron Meyer. *Aikido in America*. Berkeley, Calif.: Frog, Ltd., 1995.

Ueshiba, Kisshomaru. *The Spirit of Aikido*. Tokyo: Kodansha International, 1984.

———. *Aikido*. Tokyo: Hozansha, 1985.

Ueshiba, Morihei. *Budo Renshu* (bilingual edition). Machida, Japan: Minato Research, 1978.

———. *Budo: Teachings of the Founder of Aikido*. Translated by John Stevens. Tokyo: Kodansha International, 1991.

———. *The Art of Peace*. Boston: Shambhala Publications, 1992.

Westbrook, A., and O. Ratti. *Aikido and the Dynamic Sphere*. Rutland, Vt.: 1970.

Yamada, Yoshimitsu. *Ultimate Aikido*. New York: Citadel Press, 1994.

Most of the above books are available from *Aikido Today Magazine* Video and Book Service at P.O. Box 1060, Claremont, CA 91711-1060. Customer order number: 800-445-2454.

Credits

Except as noted below, all photos are courtesy of Kisshomaru Ueshiba/ International Aikido Archive. Charles S. Hill: 75, 76, 107, 125, 169; author's collection: 77, 93, 94, 95, 135, 148, 244 (bottom); Tadashi Namba: 78; Kumagusu Minakata Foundation: 80; Bernie Lau/Tokimune Takeda: 83, 84, 85; Omoto-kyo Foundation: 87, 88, 89, 90, 91, 98, 99, 100, 101, 102, 103, 104, 105; The Gitter Collection: 92; Misogi Kai: 114; Rinjiro Shirata: 121; copyright the British Museum: 126; Alan Nagahisa: 138, 139, 140, 141, 142; Neil and Dawn McKenzie: 143; L'Aikdo/ Jean Zin: 149, 152; Seiseki Abe: 153; Kanshu Sunadomari: 238; Joyce Stevens, 245.